Praise for Phillip Moore's
The Future of Children

"I was a student of Phillip and Karen Moore at a pivotal point in my life. They taught me the interconnected nature of science, the arts, and collaboration, which was a foundational lesson for my career in space exploration. Their love for teaching and commitment to the unique beauty of every one of their students is an increasingly rare ideology that this book puts into words to share with the world."

—Eric Roberts
Engineer, NASA and Lockheed Martin

"This book is graced by a wisdom that is rare and insight that is profound. Its pages speak to a new paradigm of educating and treating children. It suggests a New Way, an Enlightened Way. Those who dare to follow its precepts will not only transform the lives of those they teach and touch, but will themselves be forever revolutionized at their core. I cannot recommend this book highly enough!"

—Shefali Tsabary, Ph.D.
NY Times *bestselling author of*
The Conscious Parent
and The Awakened Family

"*Wow, wow, wow. This book is mind-blowing! The whole concept of the school is based on love*"

—*Ram Dass*
Spiritual teacher, cultural revolutionary,
author of Be Here Now

"*I take great joy in commending Phillip Moore and his Upland Hills Ecological Awareness Center to you. I'm personally convinced of the competence of Moore and his associates, of their integrity and of their realistic commitment to society. Warmly, faithfully,*"

—*Buckminster Fuller.*
April 20, 1979

"*I have experienced Upland Hills School and I have had the pleasure of knowing Phil Moore. Above all other things that my father was, I believe he was a great teacher. His endorsement of Phil and the staff of Upland Hills is in direct alignment with my own experience as an educator and artist. A caring-based education made a huge difference in my life and I fully support the premise of this book, which is to bring a love-based education to every child.*"

Allegra Fuller Snyder, Ph.D.
Founder, Buckminster Fuller Institute,
Prof. Emerita, UCLA

THE FUTURE OF
CHILDREN

Providing a love-based education
for every child

PHILLIP MOORE

ISBN 13:   978-0-9969285-6-4
ISBN 10:   0-9969285-6-1
Library of Congress Control Number: 2017937234

Published in the United States of America by
Emergence Education Press
P.O. Box 63767
Philadelphia, PA 19147
www.EmergenceEducation.com

For more on Phillip Moore's work: www.TrimTab.in
Printed & bound in the United States of America

ACKNOWLEDGMENTS

This book is dedicated to our children, Nina and Sasha, and our grandchildren, Sophia, Lilliya, Violet, Lola, and Knox. It is also dedicated to my parents, Harry and Jean Moore, and to Karen's parents, Rose and Nat Katz. Karen and I were loved into being and this love lives through us in every moment.

This book exists because of vision of Dorothy and Knight Webster, the founders of Upland Hills Farm. Together with a few other dreamers, they offered a place for a new kind of school to be born.

Giving birth to something is very different then sustaining it. The parents, the children, the board of directors and especially the teachers of Upland Hills School were my everyday inspiration. After 42 years of being the school's director it became apparent that We the teachers bonded so deeply that every decision, every triumph, and every tragedy were woven into a synergy that cannot be duplicated or understood by analyzing any of its parts taken separately. We merged into a larger organism that trusted the highest aspects of each unique being. This unitive being was our guide and our protector over more then four decades. I experience her as an inter-connected being who existed before we arrived and who held the possibility that this land would nourish us and teach us how to live life in a deeper way. She continues to this day and will be there for all future generations only if this unitive consciousness is honored and transacted.

I began writing this book with Steve Bhaerman who taught at our school during the early years. Steve, who is an author and coach for many writers, kept urging me to tell this story. As he and co-author Bruce Lipton celebrate the tenth anniversary of their book, "Spontaneous Evolution", I bow in gratitude for his constant presence in assisting me, and encouraging me to get it done.

I am now quite convinced that none of us does anything alone. I did not write this book as much as it wrote me. I did not make this school, rather the school made me. I venerate all teachers who teach with passion and kindness. I was deeply blessed to have experienced these teachers as a child, an adolescent, and as an adult. I am also indebted to wisdom teachers, dead and alive, who have written their words so that we can benefit from their insight.

Richard Buckminster Fuller transmuted and transformed me. From the first moment I read his words until this time, he has been my guide and mentor, my adopted grandfather and my inspiration. I have tested his ideas and trusted his integrity. I am still learning from him and will continue to until I die.

Finally this book is dedicated to Karen Moore whom I regard as the best teacher I have ever known. Her dedication to children, to values, to collaboration, to poetry and literature, to the theatre and to the magic of childhood have contributed to more then a thousand souls and will live long after she passes. From the moment we met in October of 1968 my life has belonged to hers.

CONTENTS

PREFACE

The unique patterns of sensory learning and the passionate form-creating striving of almost every child, even with rigid and conformist schooling, resemble the very impetus of evolution itself in its quest for greater complexity of form. In this way, childhood is that point of intersection between biology and cosmology. The supreme prerogative of childhood is wonder. If by some chance wonder escapes containment, the child-become-the-adult is able to respond with such totality to the incoming flow of information that he is able to organize novelty of pattern and form out of this information. Is it any wonder that so many of the great geniuses and innovators are those who have kept their childhood alive in them? Wonder has a buoyant, exhilarating, crest-of-the-wave effect. It is at once an expectancy of fulfillment and an anticipation of More to Come.

"A sense of wonder is the mark of the philosopher," Socrates once said. The aim of the cosmic questions asked by both child and philosopher is to enter into that reflexive state of delight and resonance in which one discovers the answer that tells one that the world is oneself writ large. *"I become what I behold!"* said the child-man Walt Whitman, echoing the experience of all children, as they seek to understand by incarnating the world.

The engaging, growing child is in a state of continuous creation of mutual relations with the environment. He is in a state that I have termed *psychoecology*, by which I mean that he has leaky margins with the world at large. The nervous system of a child flows into and is systemic with the systems of nature so nature is experienced sensually as self and cosmos, the one continuous with the other. Should much of this nervous system be shut down—as so much of it is in our northern European-derived education and understanding of intelligence, which discriminates against one whole half of the brain, tending to reward only left-hemisphere-dominant students, who respond well to verbal, linear styles of education—then the child becomes crippled in his critical role as a living metaphor for evolutionary striving.

We are as different from each other as snowflakes. Each of us has, especially in childhood, a special penchant for different ways of exploring our world. In order to preserve the genius and developmental potential of childhood, one must quite simply give the universe back to the child in as rich and dramatic a form as possible.

Multiperceptual learning, we have found, is a key to this gifting. In the school curricula and programs we have helped develop, the child is taught to think in images as well as in words, to learn spelling or even arithmetic in rhythmic patterns, to think with his whole body—in short, to learn school subjects, and more, from a much larger spectrum of sensory and cognitive possibilities.

So if a child shows inadequacy in one form of learning—say verbal skills—we direct him to another, in which he might find the systems of his being more readily engaged. In sensory motor skills, for instance, he may wake up and be restored to wonder, and then, as a very natural consequence, show a greater facility to learn to read and write more quickly and with greater depth and appreciation.

For some children, the growing edge of their exploration of the world is best mediated through visual thinking. For others it is through music or dance or motion. Much in classical education tends to inhibit these and frequently causes nonverbal thinkers to feel inferior and begin a process of abandonment and failure that will last all their lives. The saving daimon, fairy, or angel who could bring the abandoned child safely through its journey past the symbolic way stations of the "bad" culture is rigorously locked out and denigrated in the current order.

In many years of observation, I have never met a stupid child but I have met many self-righteously stupid and debilitating —and yes, even brain-damaging—systems of education. As we have discovered, a child can learn math as a rhythmic dance and learn it well, the places of rhythm in the brain being adjacent to the places of order. He can learn almost anything and pass the standard tests—the modern equivalent of the fairy-tale trials—if, as in the fairy tale, he is dancing, tasting, touching, hearing, seeing, and feeling information. In school as in the myth, he can delight in doing so because he is using much more of his mind-brain-body system than conventional teaching generally permits. So much of the failure in school and home stems directly from boredom, which itself stems directly from the larger failure to stimulate and not repress all those wonder areas in the child's brain and soul that could give him so many more ways of responding to his world.

With the child, however, there is always the marvelous saving grace that he is a genius at dramatizing speculation. The human child, unlike the dog or cat, acts out things that he isn't. The dog and cat don't moo or crow or whinny, (although some transitional dogs I know try.). The child can and does. Once it acquires mind and imagination, the child's body —highly sensitized by nurture, by touch, and by its still unshuttered doors of perception—lives in a state in which it is continuously bridging the psychological and the physical distance between the self and the universe.

World-building, whether it be art, culture, industry, or communications networks, is the necessary outgrowth of this special sensitivity and playful genius of the child. These extensions become the prostheses of ourselves, the further organization of nature's materials that transforms the meaning of Nature itself. Because of our neoteny, our prolonged childhood, with its extended allowance for the plasticity and playfulness of our perception and thought, we are able to become co-evolutionists and weave new threads into the fabric of reality. Herein man is evolution become conscious of itself; and in this conscious striving to join forces with the universe, our passion and our play move us to extend ourselves into novel forms on the grid of space and time.

In these creative experiences of co-evolution, we may sense these novel forms as the unfoldings of some grand design or mighty purposefulness. They are often carried in the surge of an *entelechy*—a kind of structuring dynamic energy rising from a Source that contains all codings. It is the entelechy of an acorn to be an oak. It is the entelechy of a baby to reach maturity and beyond. It is the entelechy of a popcorn to be a fully popped entity. It is the entelechy of you and me to be God only knows what. When experienced, as it frequently is, in religious, mystical, or other peak experiences, it provides a momentum for change and unfolds as a creative, transforming energy which charges one's life with growth and meaning. From years of study and observation of creative and religious type experiences, I have concluded that the process of entelechy is one of the key ways in which evolution enters into and seeds the manifest world with patterns drawn from depth levels of reality.

The child is the entelechy of the adult, and world-making is ultimately a search for higher levels of synthesis of self and world, drawn from the recognition that outer and inner worlds are interdependent aspects of reality rather than independent states. This is in keeping with a good deal of advanced evolutionary theory, which would see our body-minds as energy systems within evolution, the process that links our individuality with all of nature's strivings toward variation and multiplicity of form.

Up to now our joining of this process has been haphazard and a matter, for the most part, of chance or a crisis that leads to innovation. In the complexity and chaos of our current world, we can no longer afford to leave our evolutionary sanctions to such randomness. Here the child is father to the man; and the genius of childhood's exploration, if sustained and deepened, gives us many of the tools and qualities of mind and body that we will need to join so vast an enterprise. This is why there is so much emphasis today on embracing the inner child. For we are at a stage of self-reflection in which we are able to sustain, recover, and improve upon our childhood genius.

Recalling the world of sensory splendor known by children, Wordsworth wrote in *"Intimations of Immortality,"* in early childhood,

There was a time when meadow, grove, and stream,
The earth, and every common sight,
To me did seem
Appareled in celestial light,
The glory and the freshness of a dream.

Then, lamenting the consequent diminution of his senses, he says,

It is not now as it hath been of yore,—
Turn wheresoe'er I may,
By night or day,
The things which I have seen I now can see no more.

Wordsworth is wrong. He is wrong when he cries that *"nothing can bring back the hour of splendor in the grass, of glory in the flower."* It can come back, but bearing a different splendor, a different glory. The appreciation felt is more poignant, perhaps not unlike what the prodigal son felt when he returned from his voluntary exile and repudiation of his home. Having come back, he was given so much; his father withheld nothing.

And so it is for those of us who, in our maturity, return to the birthright of our senses. It is as it has been stated in the *Upanishads*: *"Abundance is scooped from abundance, and yet abundance remains."* There is more now than there was then. The brightness is heightened, because now the shadows are seen, as they were not in childhood. Something is missing in childhood that is given to those who make the Journey.

The connections, when remade, are now felt more keenly. The excitement of paradox acts as a constant provocation to self-transcendence, as it cannot in childhood. Realities encountered the second time around have dimensions unperceived before. Eros and aesthetic joy, passion and contemplative intelligence, give to maturity its capacities to co-create worlds that are true, and ever more true, to our inner vision of what a world can be. However, this being so, the most powerful and practical means of assuring the continued genius of childhood into the life of the child, the development of the adult, and the meeting of the complex challenges of present reality, and thus, the life of the planet is by ensuring the highest and most comprehensive development of the child, especially in his or her school days. Then, the child become adult has the temperament, the compassion, the many skills and skillful means to embark upon the wise stewardship of a world in so much need of care and radical creativity.

There are a number of schools worldwide that attempt to provide this kind of education. I have visited many of them, and some are making stalwart efforts to *"redeem the time, redeem the unread vision of the higher dream."* When asked, as I often am, is there one school that stands out for the comprehensiveness of its approach, the beauty and brilliance and sheer happiness of its students. Yes, there is. It is the Upland Hills school in Oxford, Michigan. For over forty years, under the leadership of Phillip Moore and his staff, this extraordinary school has led the way in restoring "the glory and the freshness" of the dream of what schools can be.

In the pages that follow, you, the reader will be enchanted as well as richly informed by the narrative of how this miracle has come to be, as well as how its precepts can be applied globally to a new vision of education everywhere.

I truly believe after a lifetime of working in human and social development in 109 countries that the solutions to the world's pressing problems can be solved by those who have developed the mind, body, heart, and spirit of people who have been enhanced by the methods of this luminous experiment in education. Thus, the Future of Children becomes the future of ourselves.

Jean Houston

Introduction, Part 1

THE FUTURE OF CHILDREN

My first thought when I came to Upland Hills School was, How could the children have such a good time and still learn how to read, do math, and all the other things that kids learn in school? and I spent my whole first year saying to myself, How do they do it? They do do it. They do learn how to read and write, but they do it in such a relaxed and happy atmosphere that it seems like they cannot be learning, but they're learning so much more.

—Rhea Sullivan, age ninety-nine,
former Upland Hills School teacher

An Act of Love and a Wild School

When I was four years old, I decided to paint my dad's new Cadillac. I had seen a can of rust-colored paint in the garage the day before, and I felt inspired. Sensing that I needed some assistance with this project, I asked the girl next door if she'd like to help me surprise my dad. She agreed, and the die was cast.

9

We entered the garage. I went directly to the can and found it closed tight. I picked it up in my four-year-old hands and turned it around, shook it, and determined that there was indeed something in there, but I couldn't for the life of me figure out how to get it open.

My somewhat younger friend Suzie said we had to get the top off, and that set me looking for a tool. One hammer and one flat-head screwdriver later we had managed to pry the top off. Suzie asked what was I going to paint. I pointed at the car. She pulled a Harry Houdini and was gone by the time I had found a broad, stiff paintbrush. Not to be deterred, I took the brush, put it in the can, and slapped some rust-colored paint on the lower portion of the driver's side door.

Something didn't seem right. The brush was too stiff, and I was dripping more paint on the floor and on myself than I was getting on the car. A bad feeling was rising up inside of me. Two or three more slaps, and I became sure this wasn't a good idea.

This incident is one of my earliest memories, one I remember vividly to this day. I might even say it has influenced my entire life and career.

My dad came home to find his new car ruined. He asked me why I did it, and I told him to make him happy. He smiled and said that it would have made him even happier if I had asked him first. At the time, I didn't recognize how extraordinary that response was. I didn't realize that most dads probably wouldn't have responded to an innocent yet ill-conceived act of love with a loving response. Yet, he met love with love. And no, I never tried painting any of his cars again.

As I reflect on it, my dad's love of family was always his highest priority. The patience and loving-kindness he demonstrated to me that day came directly from *his* parents. When I entered school the following year, however, I discovered very quickly that schools were not places of love or kindness like my home was, and that made me question them. In fact, I was beginning to formulate the questions that would become the foundation of my entire adult life: Why were schools the way they were? Why was everything so uniform when children are so unique? Why so much sitting, and why indoors?

And when I became an adult I had more questions, including, Why are schools pretty much the same as they were sixty years ago when the world has changed so much?

This book is my bid to change the way we look at education and the way we run our schools. The word *education* is derived from the Latin *educare*, and it means "to bring forth." Perhaps bringing forth was what schools were originally meant to do, but by the time I entered kindergarten in 1953, school meant reading, writing, and arithmetic. Today, education is equated with schooling, and schools are all about tests and funding. In an effort to "improve" our public schools we have disempowered teachers while simultaneously draining creativity and innovation from the curriculum. Teachers are overwhelmed by standards and benchmarks their students must meet, even while they are undervalued by our culture.

My experience in education over the past forty years stands in stark contrast to the schools described in the paragraph above. My experience has been at a school where every child is known and cherished for who they are, where the purpose of the entire curriculum is to cultivate the genius in each child and find ways for that genius to serve and benefit the community at large. The school where I taught and learned for all these years is a "wild school" where nature is one of the most important teachers, where children choose a large part of their program, and where developmentally appropriate skills are still covered and learned. It is a school that treats children with love and calls forth mastery. It is a multi-generational community where now the grandchildren of our earliest graduates are now attending.

I am writing this book so that people everywhere can be inspired by the story of our school and apply the lessons we have learned in their own schools and communities so that we can all prepare wise, loving, competent children for a world that needs transformation.

This book is about the future of children and the future of the human race.

Albert Einstein famously said that a problem cannot be solved with the same thinking that created the problem in the first place. Try as we might to "reform" our schools, to make them more accountable through testing, to pump more money in for technology, without an entirely new context for education, our children simply won't be able to meet the real challenges of our evolving.

As a student, I was always considered average, not very special. So it's curious that I was drawn into such a transformational project and ended up using talents I never realized I had. Perhaps being "average"—neither a genius in the accelerated-learning program or a special-education child in what we used to call "slow" classes—tuned me in to what most children need.

Children need to be seen, be heard, and be safe and protected so they can explore without danger. They need to be challenged to develop mastery, to cooperate and collaborate, to become teachers and healers of other children, and adults.

In addition to all the tangible things we want for our children, children need magic. It is during the less structured part of our school day, when children are more free to follow their interests and intuition, that the most magical things occur.

It is interesting that my own introduction to the school happened by pure, synchronistic magic.

After spending a summer in Illinois as part of Buckminster Fuller's World Game, my new wife Karen, her daughter Nina, and I took off on a round-the-world journey. We found ourselves in Malaga, Spain, which was at that time a home for many expat Americans. My incidental desire for something familiar, in this case some good old American French fries, magically opened the doorway to my life's work.

While walking through Malaga, I saw a Kresge's "5 AND 10" store, just like the one back home in Huntington Woods, Michigan. I walked to the lunch counter to order some French fries, and I stopped in my tracks. Sitting there was Ken Webster, my old camp counselor friend from a summer camp in Michigan's Upper Peninsula. When the mutual surprise wore off, we compared notes. When I told him I had just gotten my teaching degree, he said, "When you get back to Michigan, you should contact my mom. She just started a school for kids like my little sister."

And that's how I came to find the community just outside of Oxford, Michigan, that has been my home for the past forty-five years.

Upland Hills School, or as it was called then, Upland Hills Farm School, came to be during the summer and fall of 1971. It was founded by a small group of parents and educators who wanted to create a school that was free, creative, and open. When I arrived in October of that year, the school was just a few weeks old. My wife Karen and I enrolled our daughter Nina, who had just turned six. Soon after Nina was enrolled, our brand-new school began to experience serious growing pains that threatened its existence. I was hired as a teacher in December just as our founding director was fired, and by February of 1972 I had been asked to run the school.

Initially, the school was part of Upland Hills Farm, founded by Knight and Dorothy Webster in 1960. The Websters had a vision to preserve the vanishing family farm and to introduce school children to the world of rural life through a day camp and school tours. Dorothy had taught kindergarten at a progressive school for gifted children and wanted her youngest child, who was nine, to experience the best of both worlds— progressive education and life on a farm. It was Dorothy who offered me, a twenty-three-year-old with lofty ideals and hardly any experience, the job of the director. Her hope was that I could get us through the first year without having to refund tuition that had already been collected.

When Karen, Nina, and I arrived that October, we found a school of about fifty children ranging from five to sixteen who were making raku clay pots and caring for the cows, horses, pigs, sheep, chickens, and goats of Upland Hills Farm, while writing their own stories and songs. This "free school" was unlike anything we had ever seen or heard of. Located within an hour's driving distance of Detroit, it bridged two very different worlds. Our used *Yellow Submarine*–inspired school bus picked kids up from as far away as Grosse Pointe fifty miles away and brought them out to rural Oxford, Michigan. Those children from the first year traveled from the city and suburbs of a culture driven by the automobile industry to a world driven by the values of a newly emerging counter-culture.

Our school theme song was "All You Need is Love." The lyrics suggested that "there's nothing you can do that can't be done," and we sallied forth co-creating a place that was based on love rather than fear. We had read A. S. Neill's book *Summerhill*, which was published in 1960 and propounded a radical approach to childrearing, and we knew that we wanted something radically different for our own children. Neill's book, along with others written by Jonathan Kozol and John Holt, helped to spark a movement loosely called the "free school movement." Our school, Upland Hills Farm School, was one of many that formed during the 1960s and 1970s. Most of these schools were a direct reaction to traditional education. We knew what we didn't want; our challenge was to invent the schools we did want.

We didn't want schools that were driven by fear. We had all experienced a fear-based education. We were judged, tested, graded, ranked, and forced to compete. We had collectively felt the pain and discomfort of being defined and limited by the California Achievement Tests (CAT), the Scholastic Aptitude Test (SAT), and the American College Testing (ACT). But the grandfather of them all was the test developed in France and Germany supposedly to measure intelligence, the Intelligence Quotient (IQ) test. If your score on that test was average, the expectations for your future were limited to the assembly line or worse.

We wanted our school to be unlike the schools we had gone to: large, impersonal, top-down arrangements that demanded we sit in uncomfortable seats for most of the day, move when bells rang, obediently follow all directions, answer questions that always had right and wrong answers—all the while competing with our fellow classmates for the perfection of an all-A report card.

Many—most—of the free schools that began with this lofty vision floundered and failed. Perhaps one of the reasons our school was able to thrive was that from the very beginning we had teaching elders on our staff. When we hired Rhea Sullivan to work with the children in our school who needed special help, we hired someone who was very wealthy and very wise. She was wealthy by virtue of her more than forty years of direct teaching experience, and she was wise by virtue of her ability to listen and her eagerness to learn new things. She began her teaching career in 1933 and taught in a one-room schoolhouse for three years. She then taught in consolidated schools for a time, teaching elementary-school children but all the while feeling a deep frustration that she could not meet all of their needs. She finished her public school education career teaching special education and after a brief retirement looked for a place where she could be with children. She applied for a job with our school because it was close to her home without realizing it was close to her heart as well.

During the years that she was with us, Rhea asked questions, formed close friendships, took part in staff meetings, and laughed often. She taught us through her example. She was always on time, quick to forgive others, deeply connected to children, and able to face hardship with fortitude and dignity. We asked her to work with the children who we felt needed focused attention in a quiet setting. She did this by getting to know each one individually and creating a curriculum that addressed their needs. In today's diagnostic terminology, she worked with a child who was on the Asperger's spectrum, a child who was hearing impaired, one who was dyslexic, and one who had an attention deficit disorder. However, in the early years of our school we were determined to find the genius in each child and to use labels only if absolutely necessary.

It was because of teachers like Rhea that we were able to evolve. Forty years later our school is not only still functioning, it's flourishing. This book is the story of how and why we succeeded, and how what we have learned can be applied to children everywhere.

First and foremost, this book is about a love-based education.

I know that the word love itself is difficult to define, but love is the only thing that can explain the desire, passion, and dedication that has animated these past four decades at Upland Hills. It is not romantic love or sentimental love; it is the love that is source of the creative impulse, the engine that drives innovation and art. It is the transcendent force that inspires us to help others and to heal ourselves. Love is at the very core and essence of the school we created, and it's the energy that must permeate our schools of tomorrow. When love is the source of a school, it flows through the people who walk on the grounds. Love is who we are when we experience ourselves as deeply connected to each other instead of completely alone.

So what does a love-based education look like?

A love-based education creates an environment where every child is treated as a genius, in the sense that every child has a gift to give to humanity. A love-based education embraces the natural world as a primary teacher. A love-based education revolves around developmental theory, the body of scientific research pioneered by Jean Piaget, who discovered that children learn and develop through direct experience and pass through specific stages not based on their chronological age but through interactions with others and the environment.

A love-based education protects, honors, nourishes, and defends the sacred territory of childhood. A love-based education develops a curriculum that is dynamic, thematic, daring, and creative. Our teachers see childhood as a time for exploration, creative expression, free play, deep social interactions, and the unfettered expression of curiosity. Protecting and creating ways for children to explore the world around them enables young brains and bodies to develop unhampered by the restrictions of classrooms and agendas.

A school that is based on love is an extension of the most loving parenting we know. Our teachers are role models for what's possible when loving-kindness and compassion are coupled with the aspiration of learning how to cooperate with, tolerate, and understand each other. Our school is reminiscent of a healthy village where the adults and the children live with deep respect for each other and the world around them. This book is the story of how we created that school and the lessons we learned along the way.

When I was asked to be the director of Upland Hills Farm School in February of 1972, it was not because I was necessarily qualified, but because the school was on the brink of going under. I didn't hesitate and jumped at the opportunity, not knowing that I was beginning a journey that would take me into a canyon so vast that it would take forty years before I could begin to appreciate its risks and its beauty.

I am writing this book in an attempt to spark an educational uprising. This movement would invite teachers, family, and friends to come together to re-invent our schools. These new schools would be based on love, compassion, kindness, curiosity, and personal fulfillment. The aspiration of these schools is to raise a new kind of child who is deeply loving, always learning, and motivated to improve and transform our currently dysfunctional, fear-based world.

Children are our future. We need children who are loved and nourished into being by their parents, extended families, schools, friends, the natural world, and their global families. This kind of love and nourishment prepares children to face the huge world better than a degree from any college or university ever could. The children—and adults—of the future are not just competent individuals; they are so much more.

A love-based education rears kids who believe in themselves and who desire to serve others. Like our graduate Jesse, who invented the bolt covers for large wind systems, or Beth, who runs a federal agency dedicated to protecting our civil rights, they will be the social artists who invent and employ new ways of behaving, using nature as their model and our global connections as their tools.

Through our direct experiences, my co-teachers and I have accumulated enough information and insights to know that children who receive a love-based education grow up to be very different people than those schooled in traditional schools. These children are initiators and deep collaborators. They experience themselves as belonging to the natural world, and they know that they must always be creative and directly engaged with their five senses. These children are forming a new generation of transcendent beings able to utilize more of their brains while staying deeply connected to each other as they grow.

In this book we will explore one possible way to restructure schools. Our journey will begin with how to develop a new way of listening and learning from our children. It will end with the radical idea that living in the present moment is an educational requirement for the evolution of human consciousness. Along the way, you'll read about expanding children's potential, creating rites of passage, protecting the sacred territory of childhood, understanding the essential importance of the natural world as a primary teacher, and how evolution and the story of the universe is at the very heart of our curriculum—as it must be.

I will share with you how to learn from children by developing the ability to listen to them from multiple perspectives. I will tell you stories about children who were discarded and labeled and then transformed into powerful adults. I will describe ways that you can protect childhood by using imaginary play in conjunction with the creative and performing arts. I will act as your guide, and we will travel together into the most sacred realm of the wonder and enchantment of an authentic childhood.

Upland Hills School grew out of an idea that children are our future and that if you listen in new ways they will teach you things that no one else can. This book is dedicated to the nearly 900 children who attended Upland Hills School, to the teachers who inspired and sustained the school, and to the parents who entrusted us with their children and believed that love is all you need.

Rhea once asked us how we could apply what we were doing to public schools. She wanted to know how we could spread this kind of education to many more children. She asked this question and persisted in asking it because she felt it was simply unfair for just a few children to experience a love-based education. She wanted every child to experience a love-based education. This book is dedicated to all of the teachers in the world who want the very same thing that Rhea did.

By the time you finish this book, you will not be able to think about education in the same way. Instead, you will know that there is a different, more vital, more pertinent way to approach the dynamic we call learning. By the time you have read the stories and meet the kids who grew up in a love-based environment, you will want this for your own children, grandchildren, and every child in your neighborhood—and indeed, for every child that comes into this world.

Introduction, Part 2

WELCOME TO UPLAND HILLS SCHOOL

Upland Hills School
Oxford, Michigan
USA, Spaceship Earth

Dear Reader:

Welcome to our learning community. It is my honor and privilege to be your tour guide as we explore a unique and in many ways magical learning environment, Upland Hills School. I have led many, many tours of Upland Hills, usually for parents who are considering the school for their children. You have come here, I suspect, because you are curious about how our school is different. More importantly, you are likely here because you are concerned about "the future of children," another way of saying "the future of humanity."

So before we explore, let's begin with some history.

Our school grew out of the context and counterculture of the 1960s, embedded in a spontaneous "revolution" in education that was given various names. During our inaugural year of 1971–1972 and throughout the seventies, we were referred to as a "free school," a "new school," an "alternative school," and by some of our neighbors as that "hippie school." These labels never seemed to fit. We were so committed to educating our children in a loving and progressive way that we had little time to worry about what we were being called. What *was* important to us then, and even more important to us now, was that we knew the old paradigm of educating children was broken and that a new one needed to be built.

While there are no reliable statistics I can cite, the year Upland Hills School was founded—1971—may have been the year the free school movement peaked, when perhaps as many as two hundred of these schools emerged across the country. What we do know is that just a very small percentage of these schools survived the 1970s, perhaps fewer than 5 percent. Our little experiment survived and thrived as if we were a new species, teetering on the brink of extinction from one year to the next. Things for us began to stabilize in 1989, just after we completed construction on our new schoolhouse.

As to how and why we survived and are still thriving today, that is the story we tell in this book. And this book is also my story. It's the story of how my life unfolded as the leader of a project that taught me lessons that I believe can inform the future of children and influence the world to come. It is of course the story of the school itself, and of the students and how the school impacted their lives and contributed to who they are today.

An important part of this story is you, the reader, someone curious enough and someone who cares enough to discover the lessons we've learned and how they apply in your life and your world—to your children, grandchildren, and their children. So let me just say that although you could be anybody, I have the intuitive sense that you are courageous and open-minded. Like so many of the adults I have met as a gatekeeper for our learning community, you probably bring with you the courage to do your own thinking. Perhaps you think back to your own education and wonder what might have been had that education had been true to its root word—*educare*, to bring forth. What if your education had actually brought forth your unique genius, and provided a community where you could offer your gifts? What if that education honored all the intelligences, and not just the three R's? What if the fundamental context for that education was love—not just the concept or sentiment, but love that could actually be felt through the children's interaction with each other, with adults, and with nature?

If you actually enjoyed such an education, you are in a blessed minority. This book is a gateway to providing that opportunity to more and more and more of our children.

While many if not most of the "free schools" that emerged in the late 1960s and early 1970s prided themselves on their lack of structure, the success of our school is based on having found the "right" structures—the ones that simultaneously offer children the most freedom, and the ways to pursue that freedom safely.

So . . . let me take you on a tour of our school, both the physical facility and the other less visible structures that have become a container for love-based teaching, and for children to uncover, appreciate and cultivate their unique genius and gifts.

We are a relatively small school, where each child can be "known." Presently there are ninety students enrolled in our school, and they are divided into six morning-meeting groups. Each morning-meeting group has a lead teacher, and each of the groups is known by that teacher's first name (e.g., Phil's group, Ted's group, Karen's group). The average size of the groups is sixteen students, so you could say that the teacher-to-student ratio is 1:16, and that would be only partially true. We structured the school so that our youngest group, who we currently call Melissa's group, has fewer students than our oldest group, Dom's group. That's because we determined very early on that the young ones needed more attention so that they could more easily make the transition from their home or preschool to the village we call Upland Hills School. We ask a lot of our smallest children. The school day is very active, and they get to choose from a wide variety of classes. We've recently added a rest hour for the five youngest kids, and we have structured their day so that they would have more care and guidance from three adults, one full time and two part time.

If you are visiting in the morning, you are likely to see children clustered in these morning-meeting groups, either inside the classroom or outside. Morning meetings are developmentally organized, and you'll learn a lot more about that when you read chapters three and four. For now, consider them core groups focused on learning and getting along with each other as if they were a small tribe led by a wise and compassionate leader. On the older end of our school community, you might be tempted to say that Dom's group is the seventh and eighth grade, which currently has seventeen students in it, but that again would only be partially true. Lori's group could be thought of as the fifth and sixth grade, yet the beauty of a developmentally organized school is that we have the ability to closely observe each child and to place them according to their specific learning profile so that they will flourish. Each morning-meeting group meets as soon as the child arrives for one hour and forty-five minutes every day, every week for the three trimesters.

We teach math and logic by dividing into nine groups for fifty minutes every day, after a short break when the morning meeting concludes. We structured our mathematics-logics classes this way to insure consistency and practice. Every year we graduate kids who have completed Algebra One and sometimes Algebra Two. We also use this time to explore and develop every child's ability to learn independent thinking and problem solving. This concludes the morning, and the children have time to go outside for a break before lunch.

If it's lunch hour on a nice day—and sometimes even on a rainy day—children are outside, playing after lunch. The outdoors—what we call "sky time"—is one of our most valuable teachers. Children can be alone in nature and quiet. Or they can be in groups being as noisy as they choose; the outdoors absorbs their noise into its silence.

Before we begin the afternoon program, the children come back into their morning-meeting groups and spend about fifteen minutes reading quietly or with their reading partners. Some groups have established one day every week for an older child to read with a younger child, developing a close intimate relationship between older and younger kids.

There are two one-hour classes every afternoon. We use the seasons to divide the year and integrate the season into the choice of afternoon classes. For example, our school is located on a farm, and on that farm—now I'm beginning to sound like Old MacDonald—there is a community-supported agriculture plot. Every week during the fall there will be a class called Community-Supported Agriculture (CSA), open to children of all ages. One day they will work in the garden and harvest the food; the next day they cook and prepare food for the entire school for the ten weeks of fall. Another fall class is called Trail Blazers, also open to all ages. In Trail Blazers, our children mark, hike, improve, and discover the trails on our school property, which is thirty-two acres, plus a much wider area thanks to our close relationships with St. Benedict Monastery, Upland Hills Farm, Bald Mountain Recreation Area, and Addison Oaks County Park.

The afternoon program offers six choices each hour, twelve choices a day for each day of the week, giving each child a chance to take ten classes each week for the entire trimester. These are direct experiences designed to broaden, delight, inspire, and develop skills, and they also require each child to make decisions and to accept full responsibility for completing each class. We also designed a program called the Renaissance Program where at the very end of our school year we gather as an entire community to celebrate and honor the kids who have earned their Young Renaissance title, or their Renaissance, Advanced Renaissance, Leonardo, or Queen Elizabeth award. Each of these achievements requires that a student earn a credit in each one of the areas of inquiry included in the afternoon program: natural science, applied science, the creative and performing arts, community service, independent study, and physical education.

We also empower our teachers to find ways to offer a free hour to their groups. The free hour encourages children to play with one another, work on individual projects, spend time alone in nature or in a quiet area of the school, and learn how to explore unstructured time. In the younger groups, a teacher may offer their group two hours every week and help each child create a ten-week schedule where the child is responsible for remembering when their free hour is and to be respectfully aware of all of the other classes that are going on at that time. The teacher can take a free hour away if a child has behaved inappropriately.

You may be "visiting" this book with or without a child in hand, and you may be wondering how we decide to accept or not accept a child. In the early days of the school, the admission process began with a parent interview followed by a visit day. We have since added an application process that requires references and written statements from the parent, probing in-

tent. The full staff discusses each child, and together we decide whether this child and their family are a "good fit" for our
school. During the interview, the director and another staff
member take the prospective parent for a tour of the school
grounds and then to meet each teacher. We are looking to see
whether or not the parent or parents "get" the school, our purpose, and how and why we do what we do. In preparation for
the interview, we invite parents of prospective students to prepare a list of questions for us to address during the interview.
These questions usually lead us to discover any key concerns
the parents may have and to evaluate their compatibility with
the vision and mission of our school.

We have learned to listen for areas of concern, and we have
also learned how to listen for inconsistency. It's a red flag for
us if the parents disagree often, for example. Or if the child described in the interview doesn't "match" the child we see on visit day. We are concerned when a prospective parent makes demands or has lots of "conditions"; we are concerned if it seems
like staff and parents are struggling to understand each other.

We have learned to be vigilant during the interview and
visit day, and also pay close attention during the first few weeks
of the child's enrollment. As the gatekeeper I have only rarely
had to terminate enrollments —in forty-two years fewer than
six times. One was because of safety; a neglected thirteen-year-
old from an affluent family brought a loaded gun to school and
was promptly dismissed. Another example was because the
child exhibited violent, unrepentant behaviors repeatedly, and
another was because there were irreconcilable differences between the parent and the school. Our vision and mission statement is our guide and our inspiration:

Upland Hills School encourages children to know them-
selves and to connect with their environment as responsible
world citizens. We provide a full academic program that

emphasizes mastery of skills and creative growth. Our vision is that through the alignment and commitment of parents and teachers, children will come to see themselves as having extraordinary learning potential and access to the greatest human experience: love.

The mission of the school is:

To protect, nurture, and defend the innocence of child-hood; to encourage a relationship between the child and the natural world; to empower the teachers and staff; to foster cooperation and consensus in decision making; to promote mutual trust that encourages our community to form authentic relationships; to teach children how to think comprehensively; and to build friendships that connect us with others around the world.

Perhaps the most significant change in our admission process has been the addition of our website. With the advent and revolution of personal computers we developed a website that has a great deal of content. The addition of over a dozen short films allows any visitor to learn a lot about our school before they come in for an interview. Over time we have learned that direct parent referrals still drive the enrollment process. At a meeting for heads of independent schools I heard someone say the admission process is a short courtship for a potentially long-term relationship. What we've learned over time is that a great advantage of being an independent school is the ability to ask a student to leave. Our spectrum for children is wide indeed; for example, we have benefitted greatly by having a child with Down syndrome attend school with children who were headed eventually to the best universities in the United States. However, we know that we do not have the resources to work effectively with children who are severely emotionally impaired or developmentally challenged.

Anyway, back to the tour.

Our school is located in the woods. Maple, white pine, cedar, elm, ash, oak, cherry, and hickory trees, just to name a few, define and inform our daily experiences. Just across the road is St. Benedict Monastery, sitting atop a hill 1,300 feet above sea level. On a clear day we can see Detroit, which is thirty miles from the top of Monastery Hill. This land was formed about 20,000 years ago when an ancient glacier receded and shaped the five Great Lakes. It shaped the hills, wetlands, and the Clinton River watershed, and deposited massive amounts of gravel and peat moss in and around our school. We call our region the Bioregion of the Sweet Seas.

This was the hunting ground for the Nepessing tribe of the Chippewa Indians. During the early 1980s a Lakota medicine man came to our school and asked if he could build a sweat lodge. When we asked him how he found us, he said this was sacred ground and he could sense the presence of the forest tribes: the Ojibwa, Chippewa, Ottawa, and Potawatomi. Many of us, especially Karen and I, feel this sacred aspect of the forest we call home.

There are five buildings on our school grounds. The first one we built in the summer of 1972. It is a 24-foot diameter geodesic dome. We purchased a Pease Dome kit, which gave us the pre-cut skin of the dome and the plans. The rest was up to us. We finished the dome during the second year of our school with more than a little help from our friends. In 1973 in the middle of the Arab oil embargo, *National Geographic* sent the editor of its children's magazine to do a cover story about our wind-powered geodesic dome. In the early years we used our dome as a classroom, assembly area, wind-powered solar-heated workshop, and as a theatre. Today it is used as a wood workshop, math space, and clay studio. It was recently reconditioned by one of the original teachers and builders. Our dome was included in *The Smithsonian Book of Invention* as an example of what Michigan schoolteachers did to inspire others to use renewable sources of energy.

The second building, which we started building in 1977, is called the Upland Hills Ecological Awareness Center. It took us three years to build with the help of many volunteers and several paid members of our staff and parent group. This building was built to demonstrate what is possible when you integrate site-specific design and passive and active solar collectors, with an emphasis on conservation and natural building materials. It was built to house a second non-profit organization by the same name that would conduct workshops about topics that directly lead to solutions to ecological problems and to bring leading world teachers to the bioregion. It was opened in 1980 by my mentor R. Buckminster Fuller and has been used to host numerous workshops, conferences, concerts, meetings, and meditation retreats over its life span. Currently it is being used as a classroom for Upland Hills School and for workshops and tours. For over five years the state of Michigan funded tours of the Ecological Awareness Center to help spark a deeper understanding and insight in using alternative sources of energy along with leading-edge conservation to change the way we design and build buildings. Thousands of visitors took advantage of the state's support of the center, and it's anyone's guess how many of them took the initiative to build better, smarter buildings.

The third building was named by Buckminster Fuller and is known as Upland Hills House. Two parents from the school and one of our early teachers built the house. This passive solar home was built to demonstrate how a 1,500 square foot, simple, well-insulated, passive solar design could be completed for under $60,000. It is the home that Karen and I live in, and it has housed many guests and world teachers, as well as our children and one of our venerated senior teachers.

The fourth building is the main school building that was finished in 1989. It replaced the two portable classrooms that we used up until that time. A team that included an architect, a designer, a builder, and a staff member designed this building. We called the entire effort Project School House. It required our most ambitious fund-raising effort to date, and by the time it was completed we had organized several teams to fund, design, and build our new schoolhouse. For the first time in the school's history we were now under one roof. The design features a central vaulted hallway with skylights, six classrooms (each with an entire wall of windows and a door to the outside), a main meeting room, a kitchen, a library, and an office. We raised half of the funds and mortgaged the rest, keeping the entire cost as low as possible and leaving the school with a very low mortgage and little debt. The same company that built Upland Hills House, consisting of two parents and one teacher, built Project School House. The building has a heated floor, a Japanese-like main room with a hardwood floor, lots of natural daylight, and its simple design serves us very well.

Building number five is called the Karen Joy Theatre and was built to house our plays, our parent group gatherings, as well as community events that center around the creative and performing arts and larger workshops sponsored by the Upland Hills Ecological Awareness Center. From the second year of our school, the afternoon class we call Theatre Play Shop has been one of our most popular classes and an ideal actualization of a comprehensive unit that involves over half of our students to present three plays every school year. It took us until 2003 to build a venue to showcase and house these amazing plays. Two of our teachers, Karen Joy Moore and Ted Strunck, have collaborated to write almost a half dozen original musicals.

Karen writes the play and Ted the music. The most recent play, *Dreaming Real*, about two awkward middle-schoolers finding their strength through forming a relationship, opened to a full house and delivered the magic that only live theatre can.

Our staff is hired based on their passion for teaching, their ability to relate well with others, their ability to work as a team, and a dedication to continual self-improvement. The core staff consists of six morning-meeting teachers, our director, a business administrator, and a part-time staff member to assist with the afternoon program. Parents who require some tuition assistance often share in the care and maintenance of the school.

The direct experience of living in this forest and on these hills is one of peace, protection, and purpose. Waking up in Upland Hills House is an invitation to belonging. We experience ourselves as an integral part of a web of life, even when our minds lead us elsewhere. Walking to school on a wood-chip path transforms the word "commute" into "commune." I nearly died on these grounds and sometimes wonder if I was protected by this place.

In 2008 I experienced a heart attack while teaching an afternoon class just south of the Ecological Awareness Center in a circle we call the medicine wheel. I underwent quadruple bypass surgery and was placed on a heart-lung bypass machine. While recovering, doctors discovered an infection in my breastbone that required a second operation and a twenty-week recovery period. During those weeks I felt very close to death.

That gave me lots of time to review my life and to ponder questions about my impermanence.

I longed to return to Upland Hills House nested inside of a forest where the laughter of children could be felt long after the children had gone home. I eventually returned to work full time, but I was a changed person. Humbled by my brush with life and death, I began to think about the process of transitioning our school from old to new. I sensed that by the time our school reached its fortieth birthday a series of changes would need to be initiated and in place so that our school could flourish without Karen and myself.

It took a transition team over five years to develop and implement a plan. That plan is in place to this day and evolving as time reveals new challenges.

For the first time in my life since I was twenty-three I now have entered into a new stage of life. I call it my "rewirement" because I am learning so many new things that it feels like entirely new brain networks are being called into action. One of my many adopted grandparents offered this: "You are no longer being led by your role; it's now time to be led by your soul."

From my new perspective the entire Upland Hills experience has been enchanted. Finding the school, working side by side with my wife, raising our two daughters, having our oldest granddaughter attend our school for a part of a year. Working with people whom I love and admire in a place I love, doing meaningful work, are gifts that go far beyond anything I could have imagined when I began. That's the thing about being human; it is unpredictable and sometimes unimaginable.

So as our tour is coming to a close I just have to say this. You are here for a reason. You wouldn't be reading this unless you were being called to. There is something beyond our logical egoic mind that wants to be brought into being in these dangerous and hopeful times. It's a consciousness that requires us to consider that the future of our world is dependent on how we educate and venerate our children, and not just our biological children but children in the universal sense.

You must have questions of your own, and perhaps a few of them will be answered in the chapters that follow. More than likely there will be a host of unanswerable questions. Big questions. The point in me writing this book at this time is to ask us to consider—every time we see a child, every time we think of a child, every time that a child is born—how closely tied the fate of humanity is to how we raise and educate that child.

I intend that the journey of reading this book will unhinge you from prior beliefs of what "education" means and reorient you toward a future where we are more connected with one another, with nature, and with the ineffable spirit that transcends matter and mental designs. Above all, it is my wish that you recognize the love in all the structures we created at the school and in all our conscious acts and plans. Life being what it is, things don't always go according to plan. In those cases, loving intention is even more important.

One way for us to reorient ourselves is to remember our own childhood so that we can experience how different the world was when we were growing up. Considering the complexity and accelerated pace of life in the twenty-first century, we can only have greater compassion for parents raising children today. The next step in reading this book (and being with children) is to learn to listen and observe with a beginner's mind. In this way we can begin to learn from what's emerging in the present moment and to tap into our creativity rather than respond out of habit.

It is fitting that our journey in this book begins with the idea that children are our teachers. Our children take us places no one else can. Our lives change the moment our child is born or the moment we bring one into our heart and home. From that moment, we are forever changed. It is our own childhood's end, as we are called upon to serve, protect, care for another being, helpless at first but eventually to grow far beyond what we might imagine right now. That is why the future of our civilization and the future of the experiment called human life on earth are so intertwined with the future of children.

May this book inspire you, and may it in some way lead to more loving, fulfilling lives for children in the future.

Philip Moore
Spring 2017

Chapter One

CHILDREN AS TEACHERS

When you parent, it's crucial you realize you aren't raising a "mini me" but a spirit throbbing with its own signature. For this reason, it's important to separate who you are from who each of your children is. Children aren't ours to possess or own in any way. When we know this in the depths of our soul, we tailor our raising of them to their needs, rather than molding them to fit our needs.

—Dr. Shefali Tsabary,
author of The Conscious Parent

The future of children depends on our being present with children.

That's why we begin the book by acknowledging how much we learn from children, provided we are present with them. So much of what passes for "education" involves stuffing children full of information, rather than "drawing forth" who they are and discovering and providing what they require in their life and world.

The emphasis on tests, performance, competition, and winners and losers dehumanizes the very children we love. When we learn to observe, to listen, to cherish, and celebrate the innate wisdom of children, we re-humanize them. We make it safe for them to love in the world—to love their classmates and teachers, to love the natural world, and to love life.

When we recognize that children are our teachers, we cultivate the very humility that allows us to pay attention instead of pressing an agenda. We have identified seven qualities that children can help us bring out in ourselves and call forth in our children. There are probably many, many more things we can learn from children. The qualities we focus on in this chapter are: Transcendence, Deep Listening, Patience, Trust, Courage, Acceptance, and, perhaps most importantly, Love.

Children Teach Transcendence

Our daughter Sasha's birth was the first birth I had ever directly experienced. Nothing prior to that event prepared me for it. I had taken Lamaze classes with my wife Karen. I had listened to her stories about my stepdaughter Nina's birth and Karen's three days of labor. I had done some reading, and I had even interviewed my mom about my own birth, but when Karen's water broke the sequence of events that transpired literally blew my mind.

During the first stage when Karen's contractions were opening up the neck of her uterus I was pacing in a state of mild shock trying to be useful and failing miserably. I felt the connection between life and death and realized how at every moment of birth trauma and death are also quite present. During "transition," which we had been warned about in the Lamaze classes, Karen looked directly into my eyes and yelled, "Get this intern out of here! And where the hell is Dr. Lipschitz?" I felt completely incompetent, useless, and scared.

When she began pushing, I couldn't believe how impossible this all seemed and how risky. How could a human being come through such a small opening? The next thought must have been, how can mothers ever decide to do this a second time, let alone a third and fourth? During the moments when Sasha's head was crowning and she was being guided, I marveled at the skills of those assisting and at the cumulative knowledge that this team possessed. But when Sasha was placed on her mother's body shortly after the umbilical cord was cut, I dropped onto my knees and felt I had just witnessed a miracle. I was so deeply moved by Karen's courage and fortitude, her willingness to do this on behalf of new life, by her strength and her perseverance that I began to cry.

My wife and our new six-pound, thirteen-ounce child had already introduced me to the most powerful lesson that every child has to teach us, the lesson of **transcendence**.

In order for our species to continue, we must serve something far greater than our tiny selves, and we must trust beyond our reasoning mind. This lesson will emerge over and over again throughout the entire life of our child, no matter how long or short. That life could still be alive even after a child's death because as long as one person remembers a part of the essence of that life, that essence lives.

Transcendence means, "lying beyond the ordinary range of perception." Having witnessed and participated in one, I can affirm that every birth lies beyond the ordinary range of perception.

Sasha's birth introduced me to the awesome proposition of being a parent from the beginning. Because I had arrived in Nina's life when she was already three-and-a-half years old, I had never experienced the helplessness and fragility of a newborn. With Karen still in the hospital, that night I returned to my childhood home. After kissing my father and my mother, whom I now saw in an entirely different light, I lay down in the same bed I had used during my high school years. I must have wrestled with the immensity of not knowing what this all meant. I was teaching at our school and attempting to do something that had meaning and purpose. At school we were about to spend seventy percent of the teaching budget on a two-kilowatt wind generator to teach our kids that parents and teachers can take positive, meaningful actions on behalf of our Spaceship Earth, but Sasha's birth had taken me into a new realm. I was just beginning to realize how precious and how long-term raising a child would be, and I was overwhelmed with a sense of uncertainty about the whole thing. Could we support our two children while earning less than $1,000 a month? Could we sustain our marriage throughout this new child's life? Could we keep the school going long enough so that our two children would have the benefit of full-term Upland Hills School education?

No answers came to those questions and the hundreds that followed. What did begin in earnest was my own education about "leaning into" the great mystery of life and death. Our children and the children at the school were teaching us how to trust beyond our knowing. They were teaching us by their presence. They taught us by being full of vitality and by their intrinsic beauty. I remember how anxious I was while holding our child at first. I was now given this life to hold and to care for, and the meaning of my life was so deeply enhanced that I felt the seed of an awakening. We were here not only to be Sasha's parents; we were here to serve a higher purpose. Our mission was based on wanting our children to be educated in a place that was kind, creative, and free. In order to do that, we were willing to do whatever it took. That willingness allowed something beyond us to lead us, and it did. By trusting in that, we also knew we were leaving conventional wisdom behind and traveling to some other shore.

Many, many times since that day Sasha was born I have had to surrender to a transcendent power that clearly knew more than I did. It was in that moment of birth, when the immensity of life brought me to my knees, that I recognized that children bring transcendence with them when they enter. There is the classic story of the four-year-old leaning over his baby brother's crib and saying, "Tell me about heaven. I'm beginning to forget."

Whenever I begin to forget, I remember to listen to the children.

Children Teach Deep Listening

Children pay a different kind of attention, and if we pay attention we can learn from those children who seem most attuned to others, like Christine.

When Sasha was just a few months old, we installed that two-kilowatt Australian wind system. Christine, who was eleven years old, was already organizing and caring for her classmates. She made sure that when the crane was lifting the wind generator her schoolmates were a safe distance away. She had used a yellow rope to mark the line that they needed to stay behind. She also made sure that our filmmaker—a mom who had two children at the school—had a few choice vantage points with ladders at two of them so she could get it all on Super-8 film. Christine was smiling broadly yet remained very serious about her self-appointed role.

Christine had enrolled with her older sister Linda halfway through the first year of our school. Her mother had witnessed Christine hiding in a closet, attempting to do her homework, sobbing. She instinctively began to try to understand what was happening in the life of her then 8-year-old child. After several emotional conversations with Christine, and with the counsel of her more conventional older sister, she phoned our school and set up an interview.

The first time I met Marjorie, Christine's mother, she was already reaching far beyond her comfort zone in response to her daughter's unhappiness. She knew something was wrong with the way the traditional public school was interacting with her daughter, and she knew that something was unusual about how her daughter learned. She was so determined to find out what was happening and to take actions on behalf of Christine that she was willing to drive her twenty miles each day to and from this strange "hippie school."

Children have that effect on us. They force us to listen beyond ordinary listening. Marjorie felt the warmth and the kindness of our school immediately. We didn't have answers, but we too were attempting to listen as deeply as possible. We then met with her husband John, and after their children spent a visit day with us, the two girls were immediately enrolled.

As new parents to a new school, Marjorie and John quickly became ardent activists. The source of this activism and support, which continues to this day, was the happiness of their children. Both of them knew that they were taking a journey into the unknown and that the distance between their suburban home and Upland Hills Farm was not only measured in miles but in values. They understood that they were placing their precious daughters in a place that was outside of the current paradigm, and yet they were willing to do this for them.

Which brings us to the second lesson that children teach us. Children, if we allow them to, will teach us the importance and power of **deep listening**, which is a quality of being present. My dad was an intuitive deep listener. He listened without judgment and listened so carefully that he remembered names, stories, dates, and difficulties and often asked days later about someone who I was concerned about. When a child comes to me about a conflict (and I am coming from a place of equanimity), I look into their eyes and attempt to drop my internal dialogue. I often focus on the child's face as a way of centering myself in their beauty. I then attempt to listen from their perspective.

This type of listening allows us to open our hearts and our minds. The child often senses this, and something begins to emerge that comes from the connection with one another. Usually the child experiences being heard and seen, and this in and of itself leads to insight and often clarity.

Marjorie must have listened to Christine in this way, and because she acted swiftly and with a sense of urgency, her daughter deepened her trust of her mother. By the year's end, Christine had transformed from a shy, somewhat hesitant child into a bright, socially advanced extrovert who cared for every one of us. This rapid development of her interpersonal intelligence emerged as soon as she felt safe.

When the crew tightened the last bolt of our new wind system and the crane began to withdraw, our entire school erupted in applause. Christine had assigned herself the dual roles of press secretary and crowd control, both of which must have come in handy during her years at the White House a mere ten years later. Equipped with self-confidence, she was able to address her dyslexia by inventing strategies that worked for her. She organized a baby shower for our new child, and she assisted me when I was stumbling through my role as the school's director. She blossomed so quickly that we learned what it looked like when a child was flourishing.

When we teach or parent a child, we must continually remind ourselves that the reverse is also happening. Our children are teaching us and in very powerful ways "raising" us. They are often extending invitations to us to see the world from their perspective. When we accept the invitation, we see the world with fresh eyes and an open heart. We grow as they grow, and we experience their joy and their sorrow as our own. When we teach or parent a child with an agenda that is driven by our egos, we diminish ourselves, and we diminish our children. Dr. Shefali Tsabary asserts that children cannot only increase our self-awareness, they can lead us to our own enlightenment.

When Dr. Tsabary was invited to observe our school, she noticed immediately how warm and happy our children were, and they noticed how easy she was to approach and engage. Shefali interacted with such ease and interest that our children felt a connection in seconds. When children are raised and schooled in a loving and kind way, they often extend their senses. They learn how to trust their ability to feel a place and to sense beyond their five senses. It took seconds for them to know who Shefali was, and that knowing came from their ability to extend into a field of consciousness that is often missing entirely in many of our conventional schools. Deep listening is the primary tool for developing these extra senses. Sometimes I feel it's a simple equation. Deep listening equals extra-sensory development and vice versa.

Children Teach Patience

Patience is the third lesson that children teach us. Patience reminds us that life is like climbing a mountain without a top. We can attempt the climb and make progress, but we never actually arrive at the summit. As adults, we get seduced into the trance that what we are doing is "important" and that our achievements will make us happy sometime in the future when we achieve them. Children always bring us back into the here and now. Patience means taking the time to be present and to listen deeply to the child, and not the voices in our own head that are pressing some kind of agenda. Children are not the only ones who teach us about patience, but they have a special knack for testing us with regularity that few can rival.

Joey tested the boundaries and loved to break rules. When the sledding committee passed a set of rules that included no trains (two or more small sleds connected by a human hug) and no jumps, he explored some clever ways you could do those things while arguing he wasn't. My wife Karen developed the deserved reputation as being deft at casting school plays by divining the essence of a child and then typecasting them with uncanny success. She created a Winnie-the-Pooh play just for Joey to be Tigger. He was boisterous and exuberant and shared his enthusiasm whether you wanted him to or not.

He was the kind of kid that drove most public-school teachers nuts, which was rather ironic because both of his parents were public-school teachers. They knew after just a few years in his local public school that he needed something that would allow him to be himself yet help him to be more mindful of others. They were delighted when we accepted him. We sensed we were in for quite a ride, and we were right.

On a short break between our morning-meeting time and math, Sasha came into my room to announce that Joey had just taken a pee while standing on the boards between the portables. I went out to ask him what he was thinking, and he shot back, "That I was on a camping trip."

Children who are impulsive, innocently egotistical and energetic are generally medicated in traditional schools. They often disrupt class and have great difficulty sitting for long periods of time. Joey taught all of us how to work with him while he learned how to work with others, and it took four years and an ocean of patience. The key was practicing loving kindness coupled with giving him frequent opportunities to play outside.

Once Joey began to feel like he belonged, we saw gradual changes over time. It was during his fourth year that I noticed the new Joey. We offered two classes for the older children at our school called Women's Class and Men's Class. These classes grew directly out of the women's movement, but the content and the arc of them were very different. Women's Class empowered the girls to learn how to become self-reliant while directly participating in political action and awareness. Men's Class taught the boys how to share their feelings while bonding them through rites-of-passage trips.

On a Men's Class trip to the Sleeping Bear Dunes on the shores of Lake Michigan I couldn't find a father to go with me to chaperone, so I asked my dad. My dad, who had never camped a day in his life, agreed, and off we went. My first move was to place Joey in the front seat of the Suburban between my father and me. Little did I know that this would lead to "love at first ride."

My dad had recently retired and was now freed from his role as the sole provider for a family of five. In his work life he had gone from the dry-cleaning business to bar owner. He experienced abundance and bankruptcy and ended up selling paint and carpet remnants. But in this moment he could lead from his soul instead of his role. He and Joey started talking, and they didn't stop for four straight hours.

I noticed how my dad listened to Joey and how often Joey made my dad laugh. I observed how Dad delighted in Joey's exuberance and how determined Joey became to please my dad. When we began the hike through the sand dunes to our camping spot, I was a bit concerned for Dad. He had survived a heart attack, and the heat that day coupled with his having to carry a small backpack caused me to pause and look behind me. I saw Joey helping him and carrying both backpacks and Dad laughing and making jokes. "Two steps forward and one step back," he said. "At this rate we'll get there next Purim." And Joey cracked up.

That night as we were settling in, our two sleeping bags close together, I kissed my dad good night, as he had done with each of us every night of our childhood. He smiled and said, "Is this it?" meaning there's no bed, and I said, "Yep," and into sleep he slipped. I thought about how Joey seemed more relaxed than ever. How Dad's approval and acceptance had acted like a sedative for Joey. I realized that as Joey's teacher I had a large list of expectations of how I wanted him to act. I learned from watching Dad that because he had no expectations, that gave Joey room to discover new parts of himself.

Patience is a practice that requires being led by the moment while suspending your agendas and need for control. Throughout our three-day trip I watched a new Joey emerge. The conditions all seemed to conspire to allow Joey the room to grow into a person who felt connected to others rather than different from others.

At meals, Joey always asked Dad if he wanted something first, which was a complete reversal. Instead of impulsively grabbing things for himself he was more concerned for his new friend Harry. I also witnessed Joey playing with his peers in new ways, and by the time we headed home these new behaviors were working in his favor.

The year Joey graduated from our equivalent of the eighth grade he presented me with a videocassette tape of a film he had made. His film was a moving tribute of how Upland Hills School changed his life. As a new father of a young boy named Giovanni, he has relocated to live near our school. He intends to send his son to us in the very near future. As parents, teachers, husbands, fathers, and learners we often find ourselves running out of patience. As if patience were a finite thing that we could run out of. My experience is that patience can be unlimited when we enter fully into the moment and take full responsibility for what is arising in our lives. Children can help us develop the insight and equanimity that allow us to accept the moment and draw on a reserve of patience that when applied to any situation allows for something new to emerge.

Children Teach Trust, Courage, Acceptance & Integrity

Each of these qualities are unspoken requirements for successful living, and yet how often are they part of the school curriculum? The focus in our information age has shifted so much to content that schools tend to neglect the all-important context to hold all that content. No wonder we have so much achievement without deep gratification, and children at the bottom who are termed "losers" never learn to recognize the value of who they are as opposed to what they do.

If we pay attention, if we observe, if we listen deeply, we see how natural these highly-valued traits are for children to develop in themselves and call forth in others. When the school day is rigidified and the structure becomes a straightjacket, there are fewer opportunities for these traits to emerge. Because our groups are small, children can be observed even as they move freely. When we allow the "nature" in children to lead them, they may end up leading us into new territory. To put it another way, if we have an expanding Universe, why should education be contractive? Shouldn't schools be "big" enough to allow children to expand their capacity rather than just finding a place to "fit in"?

Our school setting offers multiple opportunities for children to challenge themselves and to challenge us adults to stretch to new parts of ourselves that live beyond our ordinary expectations. My experience is, children are inviting us to expand ourselves along with the Universe, the very evolutionary trait we so desperately need right now. Children learn by example, which is why adults who work with children in an authentic setting must learn and practice these lessons ourselves. Otherwise children will detect our hypocrisy, and we will lose their trust.

Trust

When we can trust the teachers at our schools, when we feel safe, then we can lean into new ways of maturing. Trust is an essential ingredient for drawing out hidden and latent potentials. Without trust, we use our cunning and energy just to survive. In a fear-based environment, not only is creativity stifled, it gets used for malignant purposes. Children teach us about trust by giving it to us without reservation. In a safe and loving setting children feel free to take your hand and to trust your kindness. Their eyes and their brightness pierce our hearts and call us to reside in our highest self. When children feel safe and loved, they can extend insight and compassion from a very early age.

Instead of report cards our school uses a process called evaluations. Three times a year we meet with parents and, in the oldest groups, with the child as well. We set aside a full hour to discuss the whole child, and often in preparation we ask children to write a self-evaluation, and we sometimes create opportunities for the entire group to offer words of kindness and insight. We discovered in the very first years of our school that even in the youngest group of five- and six-year-olds, extraordinary things can arise when trust is present.

One of our teachers gathered her group together on the oval rug in their room and asked if one child would like to go into the center of the circle to hear comments about their gifts. In turn and only if they volunteered, one by one, children would sit and listen to their classmates' comments. The teacher was astounded not only by what her students offered, but by the skillful ways that the kids chose to phrase those comments. "Tina, you are very good at drawing horses, and when you talk you have great things to say." This kind of insight was coming from a six-year-old to a child who was an introvert and rarely spoke to the other children.

Because we are all human we must be prepared for trust to be broken. It will happen no matter who you are or where you are. When we betray someone or we are betrayed, we can learn how to navigate this territory by using compassion and forgiveness.

As a rule we rarely accept a child into our school for just one year at the upper end of our morning-meeting groups. This would be equivalent to the eighth grade. We have learned over time that one year is not enough time for most adolescents to adjust to an environment that operates with implicit trust and encourages self-discipline.

During the nineties we did accept a boy into our oldest group because of his apparent sincerity and because his parents convinced us that their son needed a second chance after being asked to leave a public school. We investigated his references and interviewed several past teachers before accepting him. The other fifteen students in that group, many of which had been long-term students, made room for this new boy.

The adjustment seemed to be going so well during the fall and winter trimester that we almost forgot that he was a new student. He got all of his work in on time; he was very polite and eager to please adults; he often made comments on how lucky he was to have found our school, and his parents were beyond pleased.

In late April of his first school year, a note was found in a girl's backpack that shocked her, her mother, and then me. I met with her mother, and we talked about the horrific content of the note, which had sexual references and violent language. As I began to interview each student of the group and especially the girl—we'll call her Ashley—who was a class leader and an exemplary student, it began to dawn on me who it was.

When we matched the note with his handwriting, it was clear that our new student was hiding a secret self that was deeply disturbed and potentially dangerous. I called his mother and had her come to school. After a short time with her alone, I brought in her son and extracted a full confession.

The boy broke down and cried, begged for forgiveness, and said he'd do anything at all to make things right. His mother was devastated and nearly mute. I asked her to take him home and told her that her son was not to return to school and that she would hear from us after one week's time.

During that week, I spoke with Ashley and with her mother on a regular basis. Ashley was relieved, and so was her mother. I had a deep respect for Ashley and had watched her grow from a shy four-year-old into a beautiful, compassionate, creative young woman. I asked her if she wanted to be a part of deciding what we as a school should do, and she very much wanted to. Over the next week as a team we asked this boy to write an apology to Ashley and to the group, and we demanded that he see a therapist on a weekly basis. We let Ashley become a part of deciding if this boy could return to school and on what conditions. He and his parents had complied with all of our conditions, and he wanted very much to return.

Each week Ashley, her mom, and I would meet. Over the next four weeks, after checking in with our school's therapist and the boy's, we came to the conclusion that he could not return for the senior trip, the all-school overnight on the last day of school, or for graduation.

Ashley was very pleased with this, and although she exchanged letters with the boy he was not allowed to return to school. Five years after this occurred I heard from him, and he said he wanted to meet with me to ask for forgiveness. On a summer's day with no one else at school we met, and he thanked me for getting him into regular therapy and back on course. He had graduated high school and was accepted into a major university.

Ashley's trust for our school had been broken. We had accepted this boy. During the last weeks of her final year, she was given the opportunity to work with us in order to repair that broken trust. She graduated our school with poise and gratitude. Her senior project was a book of poetry and drawings about a shy little girl growing into a strong young person. Her book was so beautifully constructed that we posted it on our website. Ashley taught her mother, her classmates, and me about trust and how to face betrayal by staying in relationship. By choosing relationship over the hurt of betrayal, Ashley and her parents were teaching us all a lesson for the rest of our lives.

Courage
Children teach us courage by their willingness to try new things and by their ability to deal with the vicissitudes of life. They do this every day. In an environment where trust is present and where loving kindness is valued, children teach us how willing they are to take risks and to learn by making mistakes.

In 1988 our school installed something we called "the adventure playground." Inspired by a ropes course I experienced in Canada, I asked its designer, John Swain, to help us construct one here at Upland Hills School. For those of you not familiar with these courses, they were conceived of by a former Outward Bound instructor named Karl Rohnke. Karl is a key player in the field of experiential, adventure-based education. These courses encourage us to co-operate, support, and empower each other as we navigate the various elements. Each course is unique, and ours incorporated the trees and hillside just north of Grasshopper Hill.

John and his team helped us build a course where courage and trust are just as important as the skill it takes to navigate around the course. The brilliance of these courses lies in the fact that they are safer than many swing sets, yet the perceived risk seems much higher. For instance, to be able to zip across our basketball court and the swamp, a distance of about fifty yards, twenty feet above the ground, the zipper must climb a tree ladder with mountaineering gear and safety lines, cross a cable bridge, and sit on a perch before actually zipping. Once there, the trained student assistant connects the safety clips and gives instructions, and then only if the zipper agrees she gets to fly.

This course has given us the perfect opportunity to observe the courage it takes to let go. For just over twenty-five years I have had a ringside seat assisting and co-creating the conditions for children to soar. One of our former students was so taken by his experience of learning and teaching others on the adventure playground he became an avid mountaineer and climbing instructor.

Alissa used the course to teach us about overcoming disease and uncertainty. Alissa loves the ropes course even though her body sometimes makes it almost impossible for her to walk. The first time she zipped she had many fears to overcome, but when she was finally ready she flew and with that flight gained a new kind of confidence. She would need that confidence to fight the complicated disease that affects her body and has hospitalized her for many months at a time. Her teacher Jan, who loves astronomy, taught a comprehensive unit on outer space about the same time she learned to zip. Alissa was captivated by this unit of study and especially by the courage of the astronauts.

She has used her love for the stars and her courage to fly to work for NASA for a short time. As a young adult she continues to teach us by overcoming obstacles and fighting through her resistance. It seems she has learned to use challenges of life as opportunities to increase her strength.

Acceptance

Children teach us to accept life on its own terms. They seem to know that love is not something that is given or taken away by another, but is created from within. Living 170 days every year for over four decades with children has taught me something about going with the flow. They are constant reminders of resiliency.

Two children who have been teachers for our entire learning community are David and Magara. David attended school during the seventies and Magara for the last six years. Both of these children have taught us about acceptance. David grew up around the block from my childhood home in Huntington Woods, Michigan. His parents knew my parents, and his brothers were friends of my brothers and myself. David has mosaic Down syndrome. Magara also has Down syndrome.

David was the catalyst for his mother to break from conventional wisdom and to do her own thinking. She was determined to give David every opportunity to be who he was meant to be, and she could not be stopped. During the years he was with us, he taught us to expect the unexpected. He could read and write at grade level or above, but what none of us expected was that he could compose remarkable poetry. His classmates and teachers learned to value his presence and delight in his point of view. He formed one very close friendship that introduced him to laughter and delight, and he managed to navigate our rather complex daily schedule with ease and maturity.

Magara has drawn children to her with her kindness and her singing. She's formed close attachments with children from every group, and these kids have happily acted as guides and translators. She is missed when she is absent, and she lights up our school when she's present. It has been particularly instructive how interacting with her has increased the capabilities of other children and brought out their best qualities.

This kind of mutual acceptance without an agenda creates an atmosphere of inquiry and exploration. With acceptance, there is a tranquility, and the field of possibility is widened. These students taught us about equal rights by allowing us to see them as people and not as a diagnosis. They taught us to value the insights and expressions of someone different from ourselves, and in doing so they expanded our worldview.

Integrity

Remember that book from years ago called *All I Really Need to Know I Learned In Kindergarten?* Well, I could say all we really need to know we can learn from children. Perhaps the most important of these is integrity. As I have suggested earlier, the trust, courage, and acceptance that children naturally possess calls forth our integrity. Just as I was awestruck at the responsibility of being a father of a newborn baby who would grow into a child, an adolescent, and an adult, working with children and being an influence by example has made me more responsible to my own higher values. At our school, there is no covering up. The children are paying close attention.

As parents or prospective parents, grandparents, or teachers, we can learn from children how to become authentic human beings who have integrity. Children do this by watching what we do and not necessarily by listening to what we say. They are dynamic witnesses to how we act in the world, and as they develop, they challenge us by noticing all the ways we are not being who we say we are. If we can let our defenses down long enough to let their challenges in, we can use these opportunities to clean up all of the places where we are out of integrity. Integrity means being whole. Integrity means being able to say you're sorry and then doing the work to heal the relationship. Integrity means keeping your word and setting things right when you don't. Integrity and authenticity are often present in children very early on. These children who have been raised in loving families by conscious parents are the internal healers of love-based schools.

Children Teach Us How to Love

Our new schools will realize the importance of human connection and deep relationships, and they will be transformed environments where the delight of friendship is nourished, appreciated, worked on, and developed. When we think of friendship, we often think of our good friends or our best friends. Although these kinds of friendships are supported deeply in our new learning communities, at our school we encourage widening the idea of "friendship" to include everybody in the entire school. Learning communities of the future will focus on working and playing with a wide variety of very different kinds of people. Conflict resolution and play will form two of the most valuable conduits for the constant expansion of our ability to include others and value their importance.

Within this new context, certain children in every group from the very youngest to the oldest will be identified as the healers, not just of the group but also of our entire community.

Young healers are easy to identify. They are kind, considerate, and show empathetic feelings right from the beginning. Their talent is in their ability to enjoy and to care deeply for others. They laugh often and are generous with their feelings and their food. Children who demonstrate these loving characteristics are perhaps the most valuable resource for our staff. They are in leadership training from their first day, and it is our job as parents and as educators to support, value, and help to develop these traits so that the light of each of them shines brighter and brighter as they grow.

We have seen many children who fit the description of the healer, but perhaps the most recent and powerful healers are the children who will identify with the LGBT community when they become adults. These children are everywhere on the planet right now, and with the appropriate support and nourishment they have the potential to heal not only each other but the planet as well.

One of our teachers is a person who was assumed to be female at birth and transitioned to a male identity in his late teens and early twenties. His journey and his life experience, his family support and his love of children and teaching brought him into our community. When we first met, I was only aware of the fact that he had taught for ten years in the British school system and was so discouraged and frustrated that he quit without a thought of ever returning to our profession.

In our initial encounter we spoke about his interest in organic farming, but our conversation quickly turned to our school. He listened with rapt attention and asked very insightful questions, so I invited him to come for a visit.

He arrived early in the morning of his visit day and by day's end had fallen in love. I observed how carefully he interacted with the children and how much he enjoyed playing with them. His quiet, introverted demeanor along with his deep interest in others won him instant friendship. Whether he was interacting with a teacher, a parent, or a child he was able to win them over through attentive listening and genuine empathetic interest.

He had just recently married and was taking counseling classes at a local community college in support of retaining his visa and asked if he could use our school to obtain a course requirement. During his visits I noticed how extraordinary he was in ordinary situations. When he was working with children who were upset, angry, frustrated, or impulsive, he used a combination of patience and clear language to resolve and empower all parties.

One evening he and his husband came to our home for a conversation. His husband is a well-respected and beloved rabbi who lives within bicycling distance from our school. They came to tell me about Robert's transformation. Their intention was to determine if it was in everyone's best interest for Robert to reveal his entire story on the occasion of his bar mitzvah (raised Anglican, he had decided to join his husband's congregation and go through this rite of passage).

I listened and asked some questions from the perspective of the "gate keeper" of our community. I told them both that I was deeply interested in hiring Robert as a full-time teacher but did not have an opening at this time. They returned to their question about Robert's story being known by their congregation. I didn't know what to say, but I did inquire more about the process from his early childhood to the present. Robert shared openly and without reservation. He was aware at a very early age that his sense of identity did not match the social role he was expected to play as a girl. He made a clear distinction between gender identity, which is about who you are, and sexual identity, which is about who you like.

They left me with lots to think about, but I suggested that we let our community know who Robert is as a human being and move on from there at his discretion.

From my current perspective I can now look back and see how often children like Robert have come into our school. The struggles that a developing child from the LGBT community experience have expanded dimensions woven into the already immensely difficult job of becoming an adult within a poisoned world. These struggles expand the sensitivity and empathy of the child, but they also threaten their self-esteem and self-worth. For many of these children this journey presents a life-and-death stress that can be present throughout their entire lifetime.

Our communities, our schools, our workplaces, and our planet are populated with a great diversity of new beings who if nurtured and supported in a kind and compassionate manner will become catalysts for the whole health and resilience of our species. It's not like we need to plan for their arrival; they are already with us. What we do have to do is recognize them quickly, love them deeply, and listen beyond our own limited set of experiences.

Children who come into this world with empathy and kindness, as well as the ability to accept others without conditions, are intrinsic healers living life with deep purpose and meaning. Every year our school has been in existence there have been a crop of these children. They have taught us all that in evolution's plan loving-kindness has no rival. They bring light and love into the building as soon as they enter. They lift others up, and they often leave by opening their arms and sharing a hug. I have seen them transform a lonely boy into a group member with one touch and a smile. I have seen them awaken a teacher out of her melancholy and tune her into her higher self. I have seen them take a boy with a perennial runny nose and wounded self-esteem from being an outcast to an insider within a year. And when they, our healers, are in need of compassion and kindness, I have seen legions of the most unlikely kids come to their aid and assistance. They are the lifeguards of our community and are ready to dive into dangerous water to save another's life without a second thought.

When Dr. Shefali says, "It's crucial you realize you aren't raising a 'mini me' but a spirit throbbing with its own signature," she is asking us to deeply tune into each child. When we do that, we are elevated out of our own agendas and into the true essence of the child. In this way, we can experience the person before us knowing that they have a gift to give. From that awareness, we become responsible for determining what that gift is and making sure it gets expressed in the real world. When we enter into this kind of contract with a child, we discover the parts of ourselves that need to be worked on. In this way the child is teaching us how to become a better person.

Teaching and learning are like breathing. You can't just inhale. Every teacher knows deep down inside that the key to being a great teacher is directly linked to a vibrant curiosity. When we stop learning, we stop growing. Children who are loved into being are the antidotes to becoming senile. They are our fountains of youth.

In the next chapter, "Children as Potential," we will go deeper into how much children "know" even in their first weeks and months of life and the ways their wisdom and loving-kindness actually emerge. When we have the eyes to see this, we become more committed than ever to a love-based education.

Chapter Two

CHILDREN AS POTENTIAL

*The times of great change and remarkable opportunity
are upon us. To succeed we can no longer go it alone,
but must partner with one another to share innovative
and creative ways in which to rethink and restructure
our individual existence within the context of expanding
global communities. To do this requires a heightened
awareness, an awakened sense of purpose, and a dedicated
commitment to actively seek out the possible.*

*—Jean Houston, a principal founder of the
Human Potential Movement, Global Faculty
member of Upland Hills School, April 2013*

The Human Potential Movement was inspired by Abraham
Maslow's psychology of self-actualization and his belief that we
could overcome our past and create a future free of enforced or
preconceived limitations. Maslow, along with many other scientists, spiritual explorers, and paradigm shifters, turned our
collective attention from what was wrong with being human
(our pathologies) to what was possible. That shift gained mo-

mentum throughout the sixties and traveled with the force of a shifting tectonic plate from then until the present time.

Jean Houston is one of those singular teachers who are able to translate the pedagogy and ideas of what's possible into direct experiences. Her talent for introducing ideas through dance and movement, storytelling and ancient teachings, enables us to imagine ourselves as greater and more magnificent than we've ever dreamed possible. When she first encountered the children of Upland Hills School, she was greatly impressed by their energy and enthusiasm. She recognized what we were doing as helping the children to actualize, in every way—as individuals and as part of a larger community. She asked deep and insightful questions and engaged fully with the children and adults in the community. She experienced for herself how our kids interacted with each other, with the school community, and with the natural world. What she saw inspired her to comment that this was truly "a school for the world."

For indeed the Human Potential Movement finds its greatest potential in our children. They hold all the possibilities for the future, and we adults who work with children must likewise expand our view of what children are capable of. I have found this expansion to be a labor of love.

Exploring what is possible with children is like traveling to the stars with the most excited crew of astronauts ever assembled. When we remove the constraints that limit a child's excitement, creativity, joy, and enthusiasm, we open up a whole new universe of what's possible. This is exactly what our new schools should be doing. To be clear, this is an art form, an art form that must be shaped by our best social artists and dedicated teachers.

Children offer us the opportunity to discover new ways of being and new ways of learning. Our schools of the future will not be amusement parks that exploit and divert the child's sense of wonder, but rather outdoor and indoor laboratories for inventing, creating collectively, and discovering. When we get it right, our children will be lit with a passion so deep and so strong that it will last as long as they live.

The best way for us to understand how dramatic this way of teaching and learning can be is to look at the children we currently marginalize and label and discover how powerful, creative, and determined they could be if only they were given the best instead of the second best.

A Differently Gifted Child: David

David grew up around the block from my childhood home. I had known his parents Lou and Clair from the time I was in grade school. His family was a part of our suburban village, an extraordinary place because of the number of children concentrated on each block and the fact that elephants, baboons, gorillas, and giraffes were an integral part of our childhood thanks to the close proximity of the Detroit Zoo.

By the time David was born, I was in high school, and I have only a faint memory of his being "different." When our school opened in the fall of 1971, David's mother came out for a visit. David came along with her, and we talked about the possibility of David becoming a student at Upland Hills School. Clair and I knew each other a bit, but this conversation brought us much closer together. David had been diagnosed with mosaic Down syndrome. Clair had done considerable research on the topic and shared with me what she had learned. She was quiet and fierce. The experts had counseled her to find an institutional placement for David, and Clair was not about to consider the possibility of David leaving home. I asked David if he'd like to take a walk, and he and I spent some time together. Clair became my teacher on that day and an inspiration. After David visited the school for a day, we made the decision to accept him.

Through my conversation with Clair and from reading and listening to doctors about Down syndrome in general and mosaic Down syndrome specifically, I learned it was impossible to predict how much or how little a child could develop. So we did everything we could to encourage David to be himself, and he joined our school community amid cautious curiosity.

Fortunately, Clair's strong intention inspired her family's support. This, coupled with a school environment where David was understood and welcomed, made all the difference in world. He took to learning how to read and write with interest and made slow and steady progress. Then one day, under the spell of learning about poetry, David blossomed. He began writing poems that dove deep into the heart. He received so much attention from his writing that he became bewildered, but he continued to write. When our school published our first calendar, David became a published poet.

When spring comes
The trees rise up
And the children run around outside
like ponies
And running thunder
—David Fishman, age ten

He was proud of his ability to write, and he was humbled by the attention, shyly glancing down at his feet not wanting to be in the spotlight. His doctor was shocked and his mother delighted. David was in the early stages of his flowering. But it was Scott—who would become David's best friend and constant companion—who brought David into our community. The moment Scott met David he was impressed and intrigued. Who was this kid who could read and write so well? How come he was always so serious? What made him tick? So Scott went to work and followed David around talking a mile a minute, trying to make him laugh and never giving him a moment's respite. David tried to run, and he tried to hide, but Scott would not give up. Day after day we watched as Scott doggedly pursued David. When Scott told David he was a detective who knew how to catch thieves, he got David to smile. That was the crack. Once Scott knew that he could get David to smile, he was emboldened to keep hammering and hammer he did.

There were days that David tried to lose Scott and succeeded, but when Scott was sick and missed three days of school it was David who seemed lost. Then the moment that Scott had been waiting for occurred, and David asked Scott, "Would you like me to read you the new book in the library?" Scott was giddy in his response, and they disappeared into a private cubby where they could read, laugh, and plot.

They became inseparable. David danced, cracked jokes, joined Scott in imaginary play, and the two delighted us with their merriment. I overheard them outside my office door laughing and whispering. I heard Scott say, "We should give it to him" and David say, "No we shouldn't." Finally I couldn't stand it any longer and opened the door and in mock seriousness said, "Okay, hand it over." They both laughed with embarrassment, and finally Scott handed me a crinkled up piece of paper. I opened it, and there was a number written on it. I asked what it was, and David said, "Scott's girlfriend." Scott said, "No, it isn't. It is Lance's number, and he wants to marry Linda, but I do too." So I took it into the office and dialed the phone number, which was missing one digit.

"Hello, is this Lance?" I waited and then said, "Good. Are you the guy who is dating Linda?" In the background I heard the two of them gulping in fits of laughter. "Well, I'm calling on behalf of Scott, who says he's awfully sorry, but he wants to marry Linda."

That sent them over the top. Until I held the phone to their ears and they listened to a dial tone.

In April of 1977, our Dodge Maxi-Van school bus was involved in a horrible car accident. There was one fatality, and that was David's closest friend, Scott. After the bus accident David changed. Scott's death had a profound effect on David as he wrestled with the fact that his friend, his very best and only friend, was dead. He fell back into a melancholy that became his cloak. As time passed those of us who knew them at their peak could sometimes penetrate David's grief. I was one of those who knew a few tricks that Scott had taught me. The one that worked every time was saying, "Remember when you and Scott took the book *The Kid's Own X Y Z of Love and Sex* on a walk?"

David went on to work as a busboy at the House Of Pancakes and to live in a group home. When David was thirty-one years old, he invited me to his bar mitzvah. It occurred on the same weekend of my brother's wedding, but I was determined to attend them both. I talked with his mother, and she told me that when they met with the rabbi, he had suggested that the bar mitzvah occur in the small sanctuary. When Clair asked why, the rabbi hesitated and said, "Just in case he can't complete his Torah portion." Clair emphatically suggested that the large sanctuary would work just fine.

The day of his bar mitzvah, which was held in the large sanctuary, David stepped up to the bema and with clarity and confidence spoke the opening prayer of his bar mitzvah. He sailed through without a hitch, speaking slowly and clearly until the final prayer. After the stunned rabbi made a few remarks about his impeccable performance, David thanked us for attending and singled me out by saying, "I want to thank Phil Moore for flying down here in a small plane just for me."

No one knew what David's potential was. Not me, none of his teachers, not even his mother. But all of us had this one thing in common: we had the patience and wisdom to let him reveal himself in his own way and at his own pace. There is no doubt in my mind that Scott played the pivotal role in David's development. It was a gift that only he had, and even he didn't know for sure if it would work.

David was an amazing poet, a good friend, a teacher, and a "walking Zen koan." He was a paradox who trained us to abandon our ultimate dependence on reason, and it was Scott who gained enlightenment. Scott had found happiness and contentment at our school as David's best friend. He was no longer a special-ed kid who thought of himself as a loser. Their friendship and their shared curiosity led them into experiencing life as an adventure rather than a chore. Both of these boys in finding our school and each other turned on, like two full 100-watt light bulbs. We can only begin to know what's possible when we commit body and soul to ourselves and to the moment. This hundred-percent commitment is exactly what David brought to Scott—or was it Scott who brought it to David, or was it two boys tapping into a loving consciousness? As Jean Houston says, "To succeed we can no longer go it alone."

Scott died, and as Gary Zukav, the author of *The Seat of the Soul*, says, he chose to leave at that moment having finished his work here in Earth School. David lost not only his best friend, he lost a spark that they shared.

David taught us all about possibility and potential beyond expectations and left us wondering how much of children's potential is lost and untapped because of limited and limiting expectations. In meeting David where he was and listening deeply, we helped him find the written word as a way to share himself with the world. We learned that a best friend could do something that no one else could. We learned that experts can be wrong and that mothers have access to wisdom beyond reason.

From Special Ed to Special Educator: Michael

Another child, Michael, was severely injured in the aforementioned accident. Fortunately, he recovered and used his potential to build, design, implement, and invent tools to bring the island of Maui into the new paradigm of sustainable living. In spite of his own learning disabilities, Michael took the initiative to learn the architectural engineering, electrical engineering, and comprehensive planning that now form the foundation of his global toolbox. He is almost entirely self-educated. Michael had to learn from a very early age how to overcome obstacles in order to accomplish his life's purpose.

As a seven-year-old student in special education, he was labeled with severe learning disabilities. He had difficulty with letter reversals, with organizational skills, with paying attention to his teachers, and with the way he was being treated and taught. In his words, "They were trying to beat it into me." When he came to Upland Hills School, we quickly saw his genius for inventing and for collaboration. Because we have a hands-on, tool-based curriculum where half of every day can be spent in the natural world, Michael sprouted wings very quickly. He discovered that if he was passionate about something and he needed to read more about it, he was able to use the fire of his passion to learn whatever he needed to learn. He knew that if he were motivated nothing would stand in his way.

When Michael was in my morning meeting, which developmentally included fifth and sixth graders, he surprised himself, his parents, and me with his final report. At the end of his first full year of our school he handed in a hefty (twelve pages?) paper entitled, "How to Recondition Player Pianos." He had written at least eight pages of text and included drawings, charts, and diagrams. It was an amazing accomplishment by someone who was told he couldn't read or write. But what was even more compelling was that with the aid of his father he had actually reconditioned a player piano.

He is currently at the epicenter of sustainable practices as they interface with large utility companies, local building codes, state incentives, and regulations. His practice and his clients have challenged the status quo and pioneered and developed solutions that are on the leading edge of what's possible. He is confident that Maui could not only produce all of its energy needs via sustainable sources—the sun, the wind, geothermal, and wave action—he is certain that they could also export energy to the island of Oahu.

What excites me most about Michael is how he's affecting the world with his playful, charismatic attitude. He loves solving complicated problems and views his life as a huge project that will always be under construction. His wife Sabrina, who like Michael is a designer and engineer, complements Michael by bringing her formal training to bear. A native of Turkey who excelled in school, she and Michael have plans to own and operate the first totally sustainable hotel on the coast of Turkey. Meanwhile they are study partners as they prepare to take Hawaii's architect examination, but Michael knows better than most that a test result is nothing compared to the determination to make the world a better place.

A Teacher's Potential to Tap
A Child's Potential

As the 1990s opened at Upland Hills School, there was a feeling of accomplishment and fulfillment that permeated our campus. We had just completed our new school building and our first successful capital campaign. Ted Strunck came on board and quickly demonstrated his skill as a full-time staff member. We had come through a difficult decade where our enrollment shrunk to its lowest since we opened our doors in 1971, and the daily challenges of meeting a budget and running a school nearly overwhelmed me. Ted was the embodiment of a new era and a new decade.

Ted was that rare combination of an artist and pragmatist, expressing both grit and grace. He showed up no matter what. He experimented with innovative curriculum ideas that taught him invaluable lessons of what not to do and what to do, and he deeply cared. He learned that setting limits and guidelines at the beginning of a school year and then easing them as trust was built was far better than doing it the other way around. He also learned that performing the water cycle (how water moves above, on and through the earth) by giving each kid a role and engaging their creativity and imaginations was far superior than reading any book. By 1992 he was inspired to create a comprehensive unit that would culminate in the construction of a pedestrian bridge that would transform our physical plant and inspire students and teachers to reach across our perceived limitations.

Ted found the perfect fit with our oldest group. This was the group that I taught for many years, and I realized very early on that if this group of thirteen- and fourteen-year-olds were thriving, the entire school would thrive. The older kids set the tone for the school because of their energy and their size. They are, after all, the "big kids." When they are kind and excited, playful and thoughtful, the entire school follows their example; when they're self-absorbed, alienated, morose, and narcissistic, everyone feels that as well. When I asked Ted to take this group, I knew in my bones that I was doing exactly what my mentor Buckminster Fuller would do. When you find someone who can do what you are doing better than you, get out of the way.

That spring day in 1992 Ted and I went for a walk that started at his classroom and ended up at Prince Lake, a mile and a half south of the school. He told me he had this idea to build a bridge that would stretch over a valley to connect our school building to our Ecological Awareness Center. The bridge would span over 160 feet, with a height of almost 20 feet at its center. Ted spoke of a post-and-beam construction and how it would connect and integrate our campus. Years later when he was being interviewed for a short film on the bridge, he confessed that during his first year teaching middle school age kids he was a little bit fearful. The bridge was his way of keeping them outside for most of the day, with the added benefit of tiring them out. In any case, he was captivated by this idea and had already begun to research and design it. We discussed the safety, cost, and the sheer audacity of the project. I told him we didn't have the money, and he looked at me with his wry smile and said, "Okay, I'll take that as a tentative yes." I don't remember saying anything after that.

The next morning during his morning meeting he shared his vision with the kids and within that first classroom discussion heard sounds of excitement, seasoned with words of doubt. He carefully conducted these classroom discussions to build trust, to listen deeply to each student, and to explore the big questions that were arising: Why should we do this? What will it take? What do we need to learn? Will there be a role for every kid in the class? And . . . what if we fail?

During the final phase of completing the bridge, we witnessed the miracle of attempting to do the impossible. Every child, every teacher, our parent group, and one very special grandparent joined together to make an idea real. From the doubting Nicholas who transformed into the hardest worker to Grandpa Bud who taught us all how to plant utility poles by hand instead of by machine, we participated in the human miracle of true collaboration for the benefit of all.

The bridge builders of 1992–1993 experienced the power of what they were capable of, the power of potential. The actual final bolts and cross ties that finished the bridge were done without ceremony, just as tasks that needed to be completed.

In our wild schools of the future we will need to have wild teachers like Ted. These teachers will be extraordinary because instead of being steeped in lesson plans, technology, and administering tests they will have to be masters of self-actualization and collective actualization. Teachers who are able to excite, motivate, and draw out a child's potential will be the new midwives of higher consciousness.

Ted's most powerful gift is his ability to love and be loved by adolescents. He does this by being open-minded and open hearted. He listens to children, and he respects and admires them. He is fascinated by the kids in his group, and he has the ability to see each one's potential and draw it out.

Besides having his teaching degree, Ted is a professional musician and a licensed builder. Adolescents in our new postmodern world are in great need of being heard and understood. This takes patience and creative skills for sure, but it really helps if you can play a guitar and you know how to build a bridge!

When I first interviewed Ted, what struck me most was how easy it was to enjoy his company. His smile, curious nature, and infectious laugh convey a deep sense of inner confidence and high self-esteem. Working with him is so much fun because he is a "goal-oriented collaborator." As a builder, he is used to building things while problem-solving, resulting in an artifact that serves a purpose and validates completion. Ted intuitively understands that learning and being a lifelong learner is where all the juice is. Education in the current paradigm is something you "get"—a lesson, a grade, or a degree. In the new paradigm, learning how to learn and never losing the excitement and desire of learning is our deepest intention.

Early in our school's history, we came up with the idea of the "comprehensive unit" as a way of weaving various subject areas—language arts, history, science, music and art, and experiential learning—around one comprehensive theme. This idea arose out of the writings of Buckminster Fuller and in response to the fragmented ways most schools are structured, along with the need to connect the teacher's passion to the subject being taught. Every morning-meeting teacher was asked to come up with a thematic unit that ignited their interests and stirred the imaginations of the children in their group. We used time in our staff meetings to discuss how to broaden and deepen each other's comprehensive unit, and we attempted to connect our entire school through some of these units. It was one of the most dynamic ways that we used to explore a new paradigm of learning. Just by integrating separate subject areas into a whole unit we changed the game of what and how to teach. We were challenging ourselves, and the children, to think and behave "holistically," and through this practice we expanded our view of what's possible. This set the stage for Ted to lead us into new territory.

One of the first things Ted's students did to "bridge" theory and practice was to learn about the various kinds of bridges, collect images of them, and find out some of their stories. As students began to learn the history of bridges, some of them began to look at their world with the eyes of someone who knows how to connect one world to another. The Ambassador Bridge that connects Detroit to Windsor got plenty of attention, but the grandest bridge in our state of Michigan is known as the Mackinac Bridge, and it connects the Lower Peninsula to the Upper Peninsula. Many of us call it "The Big Mac," and our school culture has celebrated it in a song that I learned from an old camp friend. The refrain, "The Big Mac, not the burger but the bridge," redirects our attention from the ordinary to the extra-ordinary.

As Ted's group began the model-building phase and his classroom began to look more and more like a workshop, the enthusiasm of his students spilled out into our hallways and into the entire school. Then, because of our school's emphasis on poetry and literature, the metaphors of bridge building became an integral part of this comprehensive unit. The children wrote in their journals; their teachers began to see the influence of bridge building in their poetry; and the filmmakers were capturing it all as moving art. I began thinking and speaking about the idea of building a bridge as a way for an adolescent to cross into early adulthood. I watched and joined the class as drawings and models turned into digging holes and planting utility poles. Thirteen- and fourteen-year-olds were using their knowledge and energy to actualize. We, the entire school, experience a hidden transcendent moment whenever we use the bridge. This unique and universal experience occurs every day. When any one of us elects to go from the school to the Ecological Awareness Center or vice versa, we experience the engineering, dedication, co-operation, and leadership that was once a vision and now an everyday reality.

Humanist psychologist Carl Rogers believed that humans have one basic motive, and that is the drive to self-actualize— i.e., to fulfill one's potential and achieve the highest level of "human-beingness" we can. The entire purpose of potential is to actualize. Like a flower that will grow to its full bloom only if the conditions are right, so people will flourish and reach their potential if their environment is fertile enough. In the two years it took for the kids of Ted's group to build the bridge, we could say that it was a vehicle for the entire school community—children, teachers, and parents—to actualize themselves. Like winning a championship, the "potential" of the bridge could only be actualized through teamwork. As an added benefit of the bridge project, we came to recognize "group actualization" as the new model for our new schools. When a group bonds in significant ways around a cherished goal or accomplishment, a synergy is activated. This is what we experienced during the first days of the school when we worked together to construct a teepee and build our dome. It's another way of demonstrating that the whole is greater than the sum of its parts so that children learn to express their individual gifts as collaborators.

As his final act at the point of completion, Ted made a "bridge" to the bridge's future. He took a step back from the project and tried to imagine the whole of it. He examined each pole and the truss support system of the entire bridge and looked at how entering and exiting the bridge could be improved. He considered how the bridge might be used in the future and asked questions like, What kind of maintenance might be needed periodically? How would we replace a horizontal support log if we needed to? and What kind of conditions might cause the structure to deteriorate?

Prior to the ceremony that became the official dedication of the bridge, Ted introduced me to a song entitled "Bridges" written by Bill Staines. As we rehearsed the song for the dedication, I felt such deep admiration for my friend and colleague. He had led an entire community with loving-kindness, devoted determination, and an ethic of doing more with less to this shining moment. Whenever I play music with Ted, it feels like an open musical conversation that inevitably leads to harmony and transcendence. As we practiced, I realized that this was what joy feels like. It felt like a winter fire that had the potential to last until early spring. Blending as we sang the lyrics of the song, I felt that Ted had given us the greatest gift of all—the gift of creating something that would last beyond our lifetimes.

The bridge was an artifact that embodies the very best of what teaching and learning can be about. It spans a glacial moraine that was formed some fourteen thousand years ago, and the primary builders were thirteen and fourteen years old. It has supported thousands of people who have used it to carry themselves to and from two places that were built for a future powered by love. It has held up for over two decades, and it was restored just last year, but it will someday be earth compost for another era. It lives now as an actual fact, and it lives forever in the hearts and minds of the bridge builders of 1992 and 1993. They will remember for the rest of their lives that together they did something that they all thought was impossible.

There are bridges, bridges in the sky,
They are shining in the sun,
They are stone and steel and wood and wire,
They can change two things to one.

They are languages and letters,
They are poetry and awe,
They are love and understanding,
And they're better than a wall.

There are canyons, there are canyons,
They are yawning in the night,
They are rank and bitter anger,
And they are all devoid of light.

They are fear and blind suspicion,
They are apathy and pride,
They are dark and so foreboding,
And they're oh so very wide.

Let us build a bridge of music,
Let us cross it with a song,
Let us span another canyon,
Let us right another wrong.

Oh, and if someone should ask us,
Where we're off and bound today,
We will tell them building bridges,
And be off and on our way.

—Bill Staines

The Unbounded Potential of the "Average" Child

What is the potential for a child who was considered average? A boy who seemed to excel at nothing that the schools he attended measured? A middle child in a family of five who was happily going nowhere?

I am in the early phase of my "rewirement," which I prefer to retirement. I chose this word to remind myself that I was not tired again; on the contrary I was about to enter and embody a new stage in my development. I have learned over time that selecting the right word is essential to actualizing it. I am no longer the director of an independent school; instead I am learning how to orient myself from the perspective of my soul rather than my role. A key part to this new stage is to rewire my mind so that it suits this new stage, this soul stage. Anyone who has rewired a house knows that with a well-thought-out, comprehensive design and the use of all of the new tools and inventions that are now in play, rewiring can transform a house that was built in the fifties into a twenty-first-century home.

The first time I got "rewired" was during the late sixties. Embedded in the context of a generation of seekers and paradigm changers, the zeitgeist of this time led me to a man who changed my brain. A man whose story and ideas filled the void I felt having no grandfather as I was growing up. A man who was called the Leonardo da Vinci of the twentieth century. A mentor for me who dared our generation to "make sense" instead of earning a living.

When the first *Whole Earth Catalog* came out in 1968, it resonated deeply with my circle of friends and became an essential tool in our desire to give peace a chance. Stewart Brand, who put the catalog together, dedicated it to Richard Buckminster Fuller.

I pored over the catalogue and kept returning to the section that was dedicated to Bucky, his books, his inventions, and his ideas. I went to the Detroit alternative bookstore and bought a copy of *Utopia or Oblivion*. As I read it I noticed something happening to me that was changing the way I saw the world. Bucky wrote, "All of humanity now has the option to 'make it' successfully and sustainably, by virtue of our having minds, discovering principles and being able to employ these principles to do more with less." I was transfixed.

The world at that time seemed to be on the fast track to death and destruction. The war in Vietnam, the assassinations of Dr. King and Robert Kennedy, the over-dependency on burning toxic fossil fuels, the arms race, and the patterns of dominance and discrimination were vibrating all around us, and here was this man saying we can make the world work. It took my breath away. Who was this guy, and where did he come from, and most importantly what had he discovered that led him to believe we could "make the world work for 100% of humanity without disadvantaging the natural world"? I was hooked.

I read as much of Fuller as I could. Or, I should say, I *tried* to read as much of Bucky as I could because it was not an easy thing to do. Bucky's writing was filled with a vocabulary that was demanding and included new terms that he invented. I reached a tipping point when I realized I was reading, thinking, and talking about Bucky's ideas more than anything else. I soon came to realize that he was a philosopher, an inventor, a visionary, an architect, a mathematician, an engineer, a poet, and a cosmologist.

The deeper I was drawn into Bucky's work, the more I wanted to experience his ideas and test them in the real world. So, with a little help from my friends, we built a twenty-four-foot diameter, three-frequency geodesic dome in our backyard. We used a plan that we bought from *Popular Science* magazine; we bought two staple guns, some wood, and plastic and assembled it on a sunny day in late February of 1970. Before it blew over, we used it for a wedding ceremony. I married Karen Egner after living together for over a year and made a commitment to be a parent to her daughter Nina, who I had first met when she was three-and-a-half years old. My rewiring was beginning to reveal itself when we recited our vows with a few friends and family and a somewhat befuddled, soaked rabbi, as the sun of an early March day melted all of the snow that was inside of the dome making it feel and smell like early spring when outside it felt like late winter.

After our wedding ceremony, I was fired from my summer stint as a camp counselor. Ironically, the firing came after the ceremony because the reason for being let go was Karen and I living together unmarried the summer before. Being fired from this cherished job was devastating to me at the time. For three glorious summers I had been a part of an experimental summer camp in Michigan's Upper Peninsula. It was there in the wilds of the Hiawatha National Forest that I fell deeply in love with the natural world. Camp was also the template I drew on during the early years of Upland Hills School. The simple yet profound synergy of children, the wild, community, experimental ideals, and having fun gave rise to a rich environment where the entire community flourished. The previous summer Nina, Karen, and I had experienced all of this together, and it was hard to fathom us not being able to return.

It was Bucky who helped me see that it was an opportunity through reading his life story. I was deeply moved by his story of wanting to commit suicide after the death of his first child. He walked to the shores of Lake Michigan intending to "throw his life away." At the moment he was about to do just that, he heard an internal voice say,

> *You are a set of unique, special case experiences, you have no right to throw your life away. Instead devote yourself to doing what needs to be done for humanity that is not being tended to.*

He then experienced a transcendent state of consciousness and decided to devote his life to making sense, not to earning a living.

At the time I was reading this, I became aware of a World Game Workshop to be held on the campus of Southern Illinois University, where Bucky was a faculty member. A friend of mine, one of the dome builders, and I applied for a scholarship. I feel quite sure that it was because of my friend's leading-edge skills in computer programing that they funded both of us. For six weeks in the stifling heat of a Carbondale summer some forty people who ranged in age from eighteen to seventy-eight gathered to play World Game. While some of our contemporaries were drawn to events like Woodstock and determined to trust no one over the age of thirty, we were drawn to Bucky's ideas and his worldview. It was in Carbondale and in particular in Bucky's office that my rewiring became foundational.

Bucky was not present; he was off on one of his many circumnavigations of Spaceship Earth, although he left his office open for any of his world gamers to use. I took full advantage of this, and during many hours when I was supposed to be researching the weight of all of the primitive structures on earth (an impossible task), I listened to tape after tape of his lectures.

There I was in his office listening to his thinking-out-loud lectures from the prior two decades. His voice, which many people had trouble understanding, was to me as clear as the voice of a sea captain. Every day I listened to two or three hours of Bucky, and it was there and then that I realized I was primarily an auditory learner. I noticed that at almost every talk he referred to "the dialectic at Lake Michigan"—the time he turned away from throwing his life away and toward donating it. He never told it the same way twice, but it was a source of energy and clarity for him. He needed to touch that moment:

Something hit me very hard once, thinking about what one little man can do. Think about the Queen Mary—the whole ship goes by and then comes the rudder. And there's a tiny thing on the edge of the rudder called a trim-tab. It's a miniature rudder. Just moving that little trim-tab creates a low pressure that pulls the rudder around. Takes almost no effort at all. So I said that the little individual can be the trim-tab. Society thinks it's going right by you, that it's left you altogether. But if you're doing dynamic things mentally, the fact is that you can just put your foot out like that and the whole ship of state is going to go. So I said, "Call me Trim-tab."

By the time Bucky reached the age of seventy-three he had calculated that he had traveled more than three million miles. He thoroughly documented every detail of his life until his death in 1983. The World Game summer for me was a turning point. I had met some extraordinary people who like Bucky believed that every ordinary person was capable of so much more by learning to think in new ways. Bucky often referred to himself as an average man, who by the way was kicked out of Harvard twice for poor grades.

Bucky kept a record of his life that he called his Chronophile, and in it he kept track of all of the inventions and innovations that occurred during his lifetime along with his own experiences and insights. In 1927, at the age of thirty-two, he asked three big questions that were derived from his Chronophile:

First what could society, backing up into its future, with eyes fixed only on the ever-receding and less adequate securities of yesterday, do to make this evolutionary process a gratifying rather than a painful experience?

Second, what could the average intelligent and healthy, moneyless individual best contribute, single-handedly, toward bringing the earliest and happiest realization of advantage for society in general through taking and maintaining the comprehensive, anticipatory design-science initiative-in the face of the formidable axiomatic errors and inertias of academic authority as well as the formidable economic advantage of the massive corporations and their governments and mutually shortsighted foci of resources and capabilities exploitation? [Note: I am writing this just as Bucky said it, to give you an idea of how expansive his mind was and how much capacity it had to include numerous and far-flung ideas.]

*Third assuming that by competently reforming only the
environment instead of trying to reform man, a favorably
designed environment can be realized which will both permit
and induce man to accomplish the same logical degree of
physical success in universe as is manifest, for instance, by
the hydrogen atom, how then can the economic and technological capability of all humanity to enjoy freely all of its
world be accomplished exclusively by design science, without
any individual interfering with another and without any
individual being advantaged at the expense of another, with
a design that will also induce its spontaneous adoption by
world industrialization's managers?*

Listening to the man who asked these questions and trying to create new neural net pathways for these words to make
sense of them became the focus of my six weeks at World
Game. These weeks and all that led up to them prepared me
for playing World Game, a game I've been playing ever since.
But unlike more familiar lifelong games, playing World Game
meant that I would be putting my life energy to work in service
of the cosmos rather than in service of my own pleasure.

At the close of the World Game Workshop of 1970, I asked
a fellow participant who would become a lifelong friend to recommend ten books to read while we traveled. Karen and I had
agreed that if we went to Carbondale for six weeks so that I
could attend the workshop, as soon as we could we would embark on a journey. We both wanted to experience more of our
Spaceship Earth, and she had already experienced much more
than I when she attended the Sorbonne in Paris, France, while
still in college. So we co-created a bonding rite of passage /
honeymoon / graduation trip when we boarded a plane in New
York and flew to London, with no specific agenda. This would
be Nina's kindergarten year, and it would also be our collective
attempt to begin playing World Game. Our goal: to make the

world work for a hundred percent of humanity without disadvantaging the natural world; to make friends with people wherever we went; to learn about the countries and cultures we encountered with deep respect and reverence; and to discover our purpose as passengers aboard Spaceship Earth.

Fast-forward a decade, to January of 1980 when Buckminster Fuller came to our small, passive solar home for dinner. I had spent most of that decade applying the World Game principles to our small school in Michigan, an ordinary individual caught up in an extraordinary adventure. We were honored to have Bucky visit us in person to dedicate the Upland Hills Ecological Awareness Center, inspired by Bucky's work and vision.

When Bucky arrived, he was tired and in need of a nap, so I offered him a couch in the den, and he politely thanked me and fell into a deep sleep within minutes. When it was time for dinner, I slid the door gently and hesitated as I watched him sleep. A flood of thoughts and emotions erupted inside of me as I knelt down near his head. I had never seen him before without his glasses. I then remembered that he was born farsighted and only saw large patterns until he was fitted for glasses at the age of five. When he put his glasses on, he saw a human eye for the first time, and he never forgot the wonder of that moment. I gently kissed him on his forehead. His eyes opened immediately as he spoke the name of his beloved wife, Anne.

That night at dinner Bucky and my father sat on either side of our daughter Sasha, who was seven years old at the time. As dinner unfolded, each of the courses guided by the advice of Bucky's assistant Shirley, Bucky and my father found themselves in a competition over Sasha's attention. They were vying for her smile, her laugh, and her approval. She was delighted, because instead of a dinner of only adults, she found herself to be the main attraction, and she loved every minute of it. After Bucky ate his favorite dessert, orange sherbet, he watched Sasha sliding and jumping with delight on the wood floor near our upright piano. My father looked over at his granddaughter and with a smile said, "Look at the shukla." Bucky, who was eating his orange sherbet, asked my father to repeat that word and to spell it. My dad repeated the word and spelled it—I'm pretty sure for the first and only time in his life—and Bucky asked, "What does it mean?" Dad said it was something his parents called him, and it meant someone who shakes with joy. Bucky took his last bite of sherbet and asked with impeccable manners if he could be excused. Our perplexed family looked around, and I finally said sure and watched as he approached Sasha.

"Bucky is a shukla, too," he said, and proceeded to dance a soft shoe routine that ended with a flourish.

That evening Bucky opened the first event at our new non-profit organization the Upland Hills Ecological Awareness Center. We began building this building the summer after the bus accident, and it took three years and hundreds of volunteers to come to an almost completed condition. The center was our attempt at constructing a building out of natural local materials and was energy self-sufficient. In 1980 it was one of the first buildings in the world to integrate leading-edge solar and wind technology with site-specific design and materials.

We first honored Bucky with a reading of one of his poems and a slide show of how his ideas had been woven into the curriculum of our school. Then he stood on a small, raised platform and held us in rapt attention for over two hours as he took us on a journey that touched his worldview on corporate pirates, the basics of synergetic geometry, every child as a genius, the design-science revolution possibilities, and how to make the world work for a hundred percent of humanity without endangering the natural world. It was Bucky in his prime, eighty-four years young, and as lucid and engaging as ever.

During his talk he looked right at me, and I turned to look behind me wondering who he was looking at. He spoke as if we were the only two people in the room. "Don't get carried away with yourself," he said. "Don't let your 'little me' run the show. You must serve only the 'big me.'"

After Bucky's talk he sang us a song he had written to the tune of "Home, Home On the Range" called "Roam Home to a Dome." Then a few kids from my group sang the Beatles song, "Let It Be." Bucky was energized by the whole event, and we talked all the way back to his hotel, and he asked me to come up to his room. I was fading fast, having taken an antibiotic to ward off tonsillitis and feeling my throat closing in. He opened his brief case, which had a folded tensegrity model and a few papers. He handed me a poem called, "Ever Rethinking the Lord's Prayer." As he read it to me, I began to sink towards the pillow. As I got up and walked to the door, Bucky said that this was the most wonderful evening of his life, which threw me for a loop. Then we kissed. As I was driving home, I thought about all of the other spectacular moments of his life that I was aware of, this a mere drop in the ocean of honors and achievements, and tried to reconcile it with what he had said.

It was when I passed the spot where the bus accident occurred that I finally got it. Bucky was living each moment. He wasn't comparing one talk to another, one standing ovation to another, one accomplishment to another; he was simply receiving love and generating love.

Thirty-three years later I would be driving his daughter Allegra back to the airport. She and I had formed a friendship, and she had just given us a weekend of her time, in service to an entire workshop dedicated to tapping into our potential, not just as individuals but also as a collective. I listened to her stories of her Daddy and found in one of them such a deep connection with the many courageous parents that I have been blessed to serve over the years. She told me how her Daddy had found a way to pay tuition for her to attend an expensive private school in New York City and that she learned later in her life that she was dyslexic but never really knew it because of the Dalton School's progressive, hands-on curriculum. She became a dancer and a professor of dance. She was the one who taught her Daddy how to dance.

What's possible is beyond any of our imaginations. When I first met Bucky as words written in the introduction of the *Whole Earth Catalog*, I was incapable of imagining the events of that one evening in January of 1980. I was rewiring then, and I am rewiring now. He gave my generation and me so much more than ideas, inventions, poetry, and vision. He gave us new eyes. He gave us a new direction. He empowered us to do our own thinking. He encouraged us to invent ways to change the world. He gave us the tools to become the trim-tabs of the next century.

And, perhaps most significant of all for the development of our school, he held the belief that each and every child is a genius. That single, simple notion may be the key to children fulfilling their potential beyond expectation or even imagination. Being involved in our World Game experiment called Upland Hills School, I have seen genius emerge from the most unlikely places—like children with learning disabilities, like teachers who find their genius bringing out the potential of others, like children who emerge from isolation to find and appreciate their gifts, and like average individuals who are inspired beyond anyone or anything they had been before.

The idea of children as potential is also an attempt to shift out of the old model of having specific expectations for our children. This shift of focus, although subtle, has profound effects. Schools of the future will be places that are determined to protect, foster, nourish, and defend the innate passion and potential of each child. These new schools will not be buried under the rubble of specific curriculums, innumerable tests, top-down constrained expectations, and questions that only have one right answer. These new schools will greet every child with open eyes that see beneath the surface of things. The idea of expectations will be replaced with possibilities. We will keep asking the question, What is possible? over and over again, staying open to something so unpredictable that when it shows up we will be transported into a place of awe and wonder. David, Michael, Ted, Allegra, Bucky, and even me are examples of what can happen if you keep asking that question.

My experience so far has been that the answer to the question, What is possible? is one simple word: miracles.

Chapter Three

CHILDREN AS DEVELOPMENTAL BEINGS

One is everlastingly comparing oneself with another, with what one is, with what one should be, with someone who is more fortunate. This comparison really kills. Comparison is degrading, it perverts one's outlook. And on comparison one is brought up. All our education is based on it and so is our culture. So there is everlasting struggle to be something other than what one is. The understanding of what one is uncovers creativeness, but comparison breeds competitiveness, ruthlessness, ambition, which we think brings about progress. Progress has only led so far to more ruthless wars and misery than the world has ever known. To bring up children without comparison is true education.

—J. Krishnamurti,
World Teacher of Intrapersonal Intelligence

The Human Potential Movement was inspired by Abraham Children are our teachers, and they represent tangible examples of what's possible. They elicit something in us that takes us back to our own beginnings and perhaps the beginnings of our species. They also engender love in its many forms. Too often we adults think of them as tiny grown-ups. This couldn't be further from the truth. Children are developmental beings, always unfolding in awareness and capacity, and ever-evolving. They come into our lives as helpless, fragile, totally dependent, wide-open, complex, evolutionary extensions of our families, and our deep-time past. At the same time, they are our most essential bridge to our future. If we are to learn how to live in a global society, we will have to develop complex cognitive abilities that allow us to view the world from a multiplicity of perspectives. All children are living proof of how every one of us must move through distinct stages of growth as we construct and develop minds that are able to think beyond either/or and to reason from a perspective of both/and.

Every child takes a journey from pure openness and dependency through several stages of maturity. There are no guarantees along the way, and there are many ways a child's development can be arrested or severely damaged. Our job as parents, teachers, and community members is to do everything in our power to protect, nurture, and guide their growth with a form of love that is rooted in total acceptance and the knowledge that they are learning and absorbing information and impressions at a pace far greater than anything we are capable of.

Children move through specific, observable stages of development, and each stage is essential to their becoming. No one can jump stages. Parents are the first teachers, and we know for a fact that the prenatal stage and the first four years of a child's life are the most significant, dramatic, and dynamic stages of life, period. These are often called the formative stages because they "form" the foundation for all other stages of growth. This is why conscious parenting is central to all future generations.

So what is the foundation of "conscious parenting"? What is it that consciously we are seeking to do as parents, teachers, aunts and uncles, and grandparents to prepare a child for a future where they will thrive? When I first arrived at Upland Hills School—or as it was then known, Upland Hills Farm School—in 1971, I had at least some idea of what this would entail, thanks to two "grandfather mentors."

Buckminster Fuller mentored my mind, fulfilling a deep longing for the wise grandfather I never knew. His declaration that "all children are geniuses" altered my consciousness as soon as I heard it. In my imagination the school that did not yet exist would teach children to think for themselves and to think from a whole-systems perspective. Every subject would be related to and embedded in a holistic framework, and children would learn things within a comprehensive context.

Embracing this as a central tenet led me to explore other teachers who were teaching things that I had never before heard yet felt a deep resonance with. One of these teachers was J. Krishnamurti, who became my second grandfather mentor and offered us another guiding principle for developing children—self-intelligence.

J. Krishnamurti: The Importance of Self-Intelligence

One of the books that my friend at World Game suggested that I read was entitled *Krishnamurti: Talks and Dialogues*. I read it as Karen, Nina, and I traveled from Scotland to Norway, by way of North Africa, and by the time our journey was about to end I had been convinced that his message was an essential aspect of the new paradigm of education. I noticed that inside of my paperback edition of Talks there was a phone number for the publisher of the book. While Karen and Nina were visiting a museum, I stepped inside a phone booth and called the publisher. He told me that the best way to contact Krishnamurti was to call his school at Brockwood Park near Alresford, England. I made that call and spoke to someone about my interest in meeting Krishnamurti. When she asked me who I was and why I wanted to visit Brockwood, I boldly told her I was one of Buckminster Fuller's associates who was researching schools that would change the world. She then asked me where I was and if I needed a place to stay. I told her that we had just ended eleven months of travel and were about to fly home from London. To my utter surprise, she invited us to come visit Brockwood for three days. I hung up stunned.

When I told Karen that we had been invited to Brockwood, she looked at me with a mixture of dread and admiration. She knew me well enough to know that my imagination, laced with a predilection to stretch the truth, might have played a role in the invitation, but she had to allow for the audacity that led to the opportunity before us.

When we stepped off the bus, each of us with a backpack and the directions from our friendly bus driver, we began our walk towards Brockwood Park. The huge trees that lined the walk enchanted Karen and Nina, and I was nervously mystified by the opportunity that lay ahead. We were warmly welcomed and shown to our quarters.

At our vegetarian lunch with the faculty and students of Brockwood, I was asked if I would like to sit next to Krishnamurti, whom they referred to simply as K. Now with barely concealed trepidation I was taken directly to K, and I sat down. My heart was in my throat. K was eating his salad. I tried to center myself. We ate in silence until he turned and asked me if I knew how to build a geodesic dome.

I answered in the affirmative, thinking about the plastic dome we were married in that blew over in the first strong wind. He said that they needed one built in Saanen, Switzerland, where he gave public talks. I froze in anticipation. Stalling for time I asked him how large a dome was he thinking of, to which he answered, one that could fit a thousand people. I admitted that I did not have the technical expertise to do something on that scale, and we lapsed back into silence.

Krishnamurti was very concerned about education. He felt that children and adults needed to break their conditioning and come to understand the true nature of conflict, which was fear. He gave education a top priority in his busy global schedule and devoted much of his time to the schools he helped to found. He was committed to creating schools that helped children and adults understand the importance of what he called "self-intelligence":

The ignorant man is not the unlearned, but he who does not know himself, and the learned man is stupid when he relies on books, on knowledge and on authority to give him understanding. Understanding comes only through self-knowledge, which is awareness of one's total psychological process. Thus education, in the true sense, is the understanding of oneself, for it is within each one of us that the whole of existence is gathered.

I spoke with K at length once again in 1981. Karen and I had returned to Brockwood Park and were attending one of his public talks. These talks were held over a period of three days, and during the laundry day I was asked to present the curriculum of our school under the title of "From Buckminster Fuller to J. Krishnamurti: How Their Ideas Have Shaped Upland Hills

School." The talk was full to overflowing, and the enthusiastic response led to an invitation for me to take a walk with K.

Thirty-five years later, the conversation is still vivid in my mind. We spoke of the importance of schooling and how to best approach teaching children who were in the early stages of their development. Still curious in his mid-eighties, he asked me what I thought was most important. I told him children needed to learn how to think for themselves. He agreed and cited the dangers of conformity and comparing one child against another. Then he asked me about the qualities of the best teachers, and I told him that teachers needed to be deeply empathetic, kind, and loving. Long before the era of personal computers, he talked about computers learning faster than we human beings. He asked what I thought of them, and I said they were tools, and like any tool they could be used for good or ill. I told him it was more important for schools to emphasize our inter-connectedness.

"Do you have report cards?" he asked. I said we were developmentally organized, and I explained our evaluation process that covered the emotional, intellectual, and physical aspects of each child. He asked if the student was present at any evaluations, and I explained that many children wrote self-evaluations, and in the older groups children were required to be present to read it aloud. Each answer I gave seemed to inspire him, and he spoke about the importance of taking fear out of the evaluation process.

As we conversed, he seemed to experience a surge of vitality, perhaps because he had just heard of a school that was teaching and cultivating self-intelligence. We fell into silence and stillness for the remainder of our walk. I too felt inspired by my conversation with one of the most extraordinary thinkers of our time, someone with a highly advanced state of consciousness. I felt deeply nourished and determined to cultivate my own self-intelligence at a higher and deeper level.

That next day K came out to the stage and sat on a chair in front of an international crowd of nearly a thousand people. This slight, quiet, eighty-six-year-old who once answered the question, "Who are you?" with "A nobody." began to speak. The first thing he said was this was not an entertainment, an amusement, but a serious attempt to understand what is happening around us. He challenged us to be committed and to take actions that would lead to the end of our need to kill one another and create untold suffering and alienation. He implored us to inquire deeply within and to experience life directly in each moment without labels, as if the observer and the observed were one and the same.

As we listened I felt the urge to find new ways to create opportunities for self-intelligence to be woven into the curriculum of our daily school lives. To do so, we would have to gain a deeper understanding of how children develop, learn, and become who they are.

The Journey from Purity to Puberty

The ten years from four to fourteen for every child are the years of formation. These are the years when a child travels from purity to puberty. It is during these powerful ten years that children learn about themselves, others, language, logic, space, their bodies, and the natural world. By the time they reach their fourteenth birthday children who have been given a rich and wide variety of experiences and loving coaching achieve essential selfhood.

Our four-decade journey of inventing a school and growing a culture was informed by a deep desire to honor and protect the sacred territory of childhood. Innovative educators and leading-edge psychologists inspired us, although we first intuited many of their insights for ourselves. We then used their science and discoveries as ways of describing and communicating our curriculum to current and prospective parents. One of our most formative teachers was the Swiss developmental psychologist and philosopher Jean Piaget.

I first became familiar with Jean Piaget while taking a class on child psychology at Wayne State University's College of Education. Piaget's theory of child development explained why I struggled learning how to read. I now know I had been asked to read before I was ready or able to, very much as if I had been forced to walk before I could stand up. As early as first grade I felt ashamed, unworthy, and behind. But after reading and discussing Piaget's work, I realized that I had still been developing my capacity to read. During my college years, reading was a mixed bag. I fell in love with some great literature, but I felt overwhelmed by having to read so many different kinds of writing, from the poetic to the technical. It was particularly challenging for me as an auditory learner, who loved learning by listening and then doing.

I remember struggling to read Piaget's writing but responding to his ideas. It was as if I needed a translator to truly understand the brilliance of Piaget's research and theories. I discovered that if I read books written by other authors about Piaget, I was able to better understand his ideas. During the early 1970s as we were trying to communicate and sometimes defend our approach to teaching children how to read, I discovered a powerful tool. I knew enough about Piaget to present his idea of how children develop, going from a developmental stage he called "sensory-motor" to one called "preoperational" to "concrete operational" and finally to "formal operational," but there were specific concepts and vocabulary that I knew I needed to understand more completely and more thoroughly.

I discovered that our school was able to rent films from the University of Michigan and that they had several 16mm films on Piaget's theories that we could borrow. Back in seventh grade I had volunteered to learn how to thread a 16mm movie projector. My motivation was two-fold: I wanted to watch the films, and I wanted to miss class. Who could have guessed that this small skill would unlock something so profound and foundational to our school and would give us a deeper understanding of the world from a child's perspective?

We viewed each film at the end of staff meetings. One of the more memorable ones showed a child given two clay balls, identical in size. The balls were set on a table in front of the child, and the adult experimenter asks the child if they are the same size. Once the child responds yes, the adult flattens one of the balls. "Are they still the same," the adult asks, "or is one larger or smaller than the other?" Piaget had developed a number of these kinds of tests so that researchers around the world could identify the stage of development of each child, based on how that child saw the world. Piaget realized through these kinds of experiments that each of us is continually creating our own knowledge, continually organizing what we know.

According to Piaget, cognitive development begins with what he called the **Sensory-Motor** stage. At this stage, from about two years old to six years old, there is only one single point of focus: the self. By the time children come to our school, most of them have grown through this reflexive stage, although some are still experiencing the world mostly from this self-centered view. One of the purposes of early childhood education and kindergarten is to help the child move into the next stage, which Piaget calls **Concrete Operational**. During this stage, which usually occurs between the ages of six and eleven, the child develops what could be called the "instrumental mind" and begins to express needs, interests and desires. This is the first stage of socialization, where a child recognizes he or she isn't the center of the universe and so must communicate her needs and desires clearly and appropriately.

A four-and-a-half-year-old child joining our school discovers quite quickly the differences between her home, preschool, or prior day-care situation and this new school. On entering our school, this new student will be guided by a teacher who is able to interact with and directly guide the child, and listen with deep patience and understanding. Our teachers use the theoretical knowledge we learned from Piaget and others to become bridges and guides for children and in doing so make the theoretical "real."

We discovered two primary issues that present opportunities for us to guide a child from preoperational to concrete operational, or from self-centeredness to otherness. These two areas are conflicts and play time.

Every conflict is an opportunity to help build a bridge. Our teachers have acquired—and are constantly revising and expanding—a tool chest to use when conflicts arise. Not only are conflicts a natural part of life, they are opportunities for cultivating self-intelligence and growth. The tools we use to face and transform conflict are designed to help children cultivate the ability to solve their own problems. Instead being "adults who know best" telling children what to do, our teachers have learned to listen patiently, to ask the right questions, and to gently guide the child to finding his or her own solutions. Perhaps the most important skill a teacher can develop is the skill of meeting the child where she is in her development and gently guiding her to the next stage. This requires consistency, clear boundaries, a kindly tone of voice, and the ability to cut to the source of the conflict, all the while using words that the child understands.

A simple thing like sharing a swing set presents a real-life situation that forms the foundation for learning how to live in a community.

When Laura first came to us, she had many difficulties that overwhelmed her and caused her to yell out, cry, or argue. Laura had been going to daycare and preschool since she was two. She had learned how to get her way by throwing a fit, yelling, and refusing to comply. Her parents wanted her to be a strong person and were ambivalent during the many times that Laura asserted herself. They mistook her demanding behavior for strength.

When Laura used those same behaviors at school, her teacher immediately went into action to separate Laura and to set the parameters without negotiation. Laura was not pleased with this. After her teacher had several conversations with Laura's dad, who picked her up after school each day, her parents and the staff aligned so that she would be treated consistently at home and at school. Throughout her entire first year Laura pushed and tested until she realized that she was being loved in a way that she had never been loved before. Over the course of months, Laura eventually began to feel protected by these boundaries instead of abandoned. As we later found out, a large part of her distress came from her being separated from her loving parents for too long.

Play—particularly when it involves engaging with and negotiating with others—is another area where aware adults can foster development. For example, whenever it was time for free play, Carol would stand alone looking disappointed.

"What's the matter?" a teacher would ask.

"Nobody wants to play with me," she would reply.

A skilled teacher would respond with questions designed to help identify the problem and empower the child to solve the problem: "Have you asked someone to play with you?" "Did something happen?" "Is there something you'd like to do?" Based on her responses, Carol would receive some advice and a directed action that could help her solve this problem.

However, the most powerful catalyst that moves a child from self-centeredness to group centeredness is the love of a friend. When a school culture embraces friendship as an integral part of moving into the next developmental stage, a subtle but potent shift occurs. Friendship cannot be forced or manipulated, and in some cases it may take a few years for a true friendship to develop, but when it does the development of each child is nourished and accelerated.

The third stage begins in adolescence and helps inform interpersonal relationships and mutuality. Piaget called this **Formal Operational**, and it includes the ability to hold many variables simultaneously and make comparisons while problem solving. This stage is usually defined by living in relationship with others in roles and rules set by our local culture. The opinions of others strongly influence us, and we often are more able to follow than lead, which is why it is often referred to as the socialized mind. At the same time, as Krishnamurti cautioned, we must help children and young people think for themselves so that socialization doesn't devolve into conformity.

The stage our school needed to know best was the preoperational stage, where children are egocentric and engaged in magical thinking and symbolic play. We had to simultaneously provide an opportunity for this stage to play out and to bring children into Concrete Operational, where they learn to think and express themselves in a more organized and rational way. Finally, we had to cultivate Formal Operational and abstract reasoning to prepare our older children for high school and beyond. When children are given great novels to read in small groups of eight, like *To Kill a Mockingbird* or *True Grit*, the ensuing group discussions greatly help in shifting the child from a concrete "black and white" worldview to a more complex and nuanced one. After reading *The Diary of Anne Frank*, a trip to the Holocaust Memorial Center can be a defining moment for many children. These bridges have been used at our school for decades, and we have seen how empowering it is for our children to know intimately a few great works as opposed to a huge variety of lesser works or textbooks. (We also discovered developmental stages beyond the scope of Piaget's work; we will say more about that shortly.)

Immersion into Piaget's work and world gave us a whole-systems perspective of how children view the world and gave me a better understanding about why schooling—as left-hemisphere dominated as it is—was so challenging for me. As a staff, we viewed each of the Piaget films, and our discussions of what we saw informed not just our curriculum but how we interacted with each individual child. After each film, we shared our viewpoints and reflections and then related these to our everyday experience. I cannot emphasize enough how powerful it was to immerse ourselves in Piaget's insights and then watch them play out over the course of the week. This marriage of theory and practice is all too rare in the everyday operations of our schools.

Our understanding of Jean Piaget's theory of developmental stages transformed the way we viewed each child. Even though Piaget's work is taught in almost all teacher-training curricula the world over, most schools have yet to integrate his ideas and the ideas of his predecessors into the way children are taught. Most of our schools are still trapped in the archaic and obsolete industrial model of education where children are grouped by chronological age. We place children in a kindergarten without recognizing or utilizing the marvelous insights of the inventor of kindergarten, Frederick Froebel, who developed an entire set of activities and investigations that revolutionized the way we introduced children into our schools.

In standard schooling, starting in kindergarten children follow a linear assembly line to first grade, second grade, all the way through the senior year of high school, in a system that imagines all children need to learn the same thing in the same way. And yet, thanks to Jean Piaget and those who have applied his ideas in developmental psychology, we know that the notion that every six-year-old should know a specific list of very detailed things is as obsolete as a rotary dial telephone.

In order to fully understand and appreciate the breakthrough understandings of Piaget and his colleagues, I invited one of his researchers, Gilbert Voyat, to visit our school. Gilbert was a professor of psychology at City College in New York City, applying Piaget's work via a tool he called "The Artists Carnival." He stayed with us for one night and one day of school that began at 8 a.m. and ended with a parent group meeting at 9 p.m.

A formally trained Ph.D. from the University of Geneva, Dr. Voyat took copious notes from the moment our children arrived until the moment they cleaned up their classrooms and prepared to go home. He watched the entire day without saying more than a few words. We all gathered around our staff-meeting table, and we waited. He looked at his notes for several long minutes and then began by saying,

> *I have never seen a school like this one. The children are so engaged in learning in all types of ways. They are productive, happy, and very kind to each other. Piaget did not want to become a founder of schools; he believed that his research and theories needed to be applied by educators. He did not want to see schools called Piagetian schools, but if he were able to visit this school he might have changed his mind.*

Gilbert's observations and sharing with the parents that evening led us to appreciate how important play is in a child's life and how essential art and music are as vehicles to selfhood. His careful account of the children's free play was filled with observations of how they integrated, tested, and practiced the lessons that they most needed to understand. He was deeply interested in how the environment at our school facilitated a child's journey from egocentrism to socio-centrism, a central tenet of one of Piaget's theories. Gilbert observed that because every child knew every other child and because they were often given opportunities to interact in parallel play or directly with each other, our children very quickly learned how to share, how to collaborate, how to resolve conflicts, how to build together, and how to empathize with one another.

The power of the ten years from four until fourteen is rooted in Piaget's theory. It is during these ten years that a child learns who she is and how to care deeply for others and for our earth. In Piaget's own words,

> *Education, for most people, means trying to lead the child to resemble the typical adult of his society . . . but for me and no one else, education means making creators . . . You have to make inventors, innovators—not conformists.*

Piaget believed that only through education could we save our world and that moral development must be led by a child's own discoveries of what is right or wrong and proceed through stages.

When we understood the depth and implications of Piaget's work, we began to trust our own intuitive powers with a greater appreciation for our own collective insights. Perhaps most importantly, Piaget's insights reaffirmed another fundamental principle of our school—love. Along with every learning theory, every curriculum idea, every structure and practice at our school was the love we had for our children and for our work with them. Teachers who are in love with their lives, with their work, and with the children serve as the best role models, particularly when children and communities have to face life's challenges that are not "part of the curriculum."

We also used Piaget's scientific model to help our parents understand the reasons we structured our morning-meeting groups to span two years and why it was not chronological age that determined their placement but their stage of development. We also learned how to observe, listen, and serve the children we worked with every day. Equipped with the tools of a developmental model, we understood that every line of intelligence proceeds from a first stage and includes everything learned there in order to move to a second stage; include and transcend became an operative principle that had universal implications beyond human development. Piaget's work gave us a map of how to understand every child's growth process.

To summarize, this linear development of what we might call "maturity" seems obvious. We begin as totally dependent, self-focused beings. We then learn how to make our needs known and move toward what we want and away from what we don't want. Finally, we learn how to operate as responsible, independent beings in the context of community. However, that isn't the whole picture.

Not too long ago our developmental psychologists assumed that focusing on our development as infants, children and adolescents would give us a true picture of the developing mind. This is not completely true. Thanks to the work of Robert Kegan and many other scientists we know that the adult mind continues to develop.

Kegan has identified two more stages after the socialized mind. What he calls the self-authoring mind is able to take a step back from its environment and develop an identity free of the judgment of others. Those who master this stage are self-directed and independent thinkers, and this trait can develop—and be cultivated—prior to adulthood. We have worked with many children who over time have demonstrated these characteristics. Our school culture places a high value on self-motivation and independent thinking, which has resulted in developing children who are able to think, behave, and actualize on an adult level. It is astonishing (but not really surprising) how a loving environment that is dedicated to meeting each child as a genius can empower children to cognize and actualize beyond perceived limitations.

The Self-Authoring Mind: William's Boat

Will had seen plans in Popular Science that detailed the construction of a sailboat using just two 4 x 8 sheets of plywood. He presented the idea to our staff, and Ted volunteered enthusiastically to be his mentor. What happened over the course of this project was so profoundly transformational that it shines as an example of how to create the perfect environment for self-authoring.

Will was a quiet, confident student who had a wry sense of humor and an engaging personality. He began working on this project in our dome workshop and from the very first day encountered major problems. The first problem was that he needed carbon paper to transfer the boat plans to the wood. Will had never heard of carbon paper. This sent him around the school asking other staff members for direction, and he found that one of his first teachers had some. Ted showed Will how to use it, and the two of them worked without stopping for hours until they had transferred the entire set of plans onto the plywood.

I stopped in to see how they were doing and noticed William's attention to detail, moving the carbon paper only eight inches at a time, along with his focused attention. William became transfixed by his boat project, and in some sense he was not building the boat as much as the boat was building him. The end of the year was rapidly advancing, and it was clear that he would not be finished by the last day. This had no effect on him. He asked if he could work during the summer to finish what he had started. He got to school day after day, by way of his dad or his mom, and worked with and without supervision. Finally with Ted and his dad nearby he finished the boat, which he had named Phoebe because as soon as they brought it outside the dome, a phoebe landed on it.

It was on a summer day when I was 250 miles away that William sailed his boat. He and Ted drove it to a small lake, gently lowered it into the water, hoisted the sail, and off he went. As Ted stood on shore he marveled at what this boy had done. With tears in his eyes he watched William tack and sail all the while in a state of shock. This was Ted's hope and dream actualized. William's determination, dedication, and ability to solve every problem, including a forty-five-mile round-trip drive every day during the summer, was something that went far beyond completing a project.

William took control of his thirteen-year-old life and authored a boat.

He went beyond the expectations of his family, friends, and subculture. He did this for himself as a test. Can I do something that seems impossible? Can I sail away using the power of the wind? Can I leave my childhood behind and take this confidence into the great unknown of what's next?

Ted sent me a couple of pictures and a short note by email. Even at a distance it produced that same powerful effect. Tears. This boy had surprised us all. When Ted retired as a full-time teacher, William came back to honor him. Towards the end of the evening a jam session unfolded, and as we were playing the Beatles tune "The Long and Winding Road," I looked into William's eyes, now a man, and looked back at Ted as we sang these words: "Anyway you'll never know the many times I've cried."

This is the gold of teaching, I thought. This is the reason we got up every day determined to do our best and willing to take risks. William, whom I did not recognize when I first saw him, smiled at me as we were singing, and in that smile I saw the boy was still there, intact. I also saw the confidence as he played with skill and tenderness. William climbed his first mountain when he was just thirteen, and at twenty-three he was ready for more.

The last stage in Kegan's model is called the **self-transforming mind**. From this point of view one is able to regard multiple ideologies simultaneously and compare them. At this level, one asks questions like, "Why do people continue to kill each other?" and "What is the root of fear?" The self-transforming mind is the creator of contexts and the seat of self-intelligence.

The work that begins when a child is four and a half, the work of learning how to live with others, continues throughout our lives. The essence of creating a world that works is determined by our ability to do our own thinking and by cultivating a true moral compass. We found very early on that when our students were developing it was important for us to create a safe environment where justice and fairness prevailed. In order to do this, we became aware of how sharing, following rules, investigating and challenging rules, and mediating conflicts all required an environment that was dedicated to care and kindness. How important is kindness? We think it is essential.

The Stages of Moral Development

Before there were "search engines," we used the word "developmental" to discover other psychologists and educators who were furthering the pioneering work of Piaget. This led us to Lawrence Kohlberg and his theory of moral development. Moral reasoning was something that Piaget was very interested in, and Kohlberg expanded our understanding by identifying three levels with six stages.

Kohlberg interviewed many children at different stages of their development and discovered clear markers as children moved from the **pre-conventional level** (stage one: obedience and punishment; stage two: individualism and exchange) to the **conventional level** (stage three: interpersonal relationships; stage four: maintaining social order) to the **post-conventional level** (stage five: social contract and individual rights; stage six: universal principles). Through Kohlberg's work, we now had a template to help us identify and evolve whatever stage of moral development our children were in. We encouraged children to listen to their peers and to aspire to the qualities at the level just above their own. We used moral dilemmas and short fictional stories to encourage children to explore their feelings and ideas, and to listen to others do the same thing. We soon discovered that in a safe environment children were able to make rapid progress and surpass many adults in their moral development!

Kohlberg's work became one of the most useful tools for me in my role as the director of our school. As director, I have been involved in most of the difficult and complex dramas and moral dilemmas that unfold in our learning community. My job, from the very first day, has been to help explore the territory of human conflict and the darker aspects of human nature, and have the entire school community learn from it. The scope of situations I have encountered range from the young child who is always "right" and throws temper tantrums that spill into violence to the troubled boy who writes secret notes with explicit sexual content and dark threats to an adolescent girl who is a paragon of integrity.

This line of inquiry, moral reasoning, is central to creating a healthy learning community. Schools have the unique ability to create healing communities. The root of the word *healing* is to "restore wholeness," and so in this sense a healing community is one that acknowledges and works with the "whole child"—not just the part of children that fits comfortably in a schoolroom chair. When children learn that they are safe being themselves, they extend that safety to other children naturally, largely without prompting.

At the beginning of our fifth decade I can report that there are a growing number of children who have extraordinary healing abilities. These children, when encouraged and supported, have the ability to heal a child who has been mercilessly teased at his previous school, to teach other children how to accept and honor children who are different, and to lead by example through tenderness and compassion. I believe we have more of these children alive on this planet at this time than at any other time of human experience, although I believe they have been with us since the beginning of our species.

We have seen how a child having a leadership year in a group can have profound consequences. Perhaps the most outstanding example of that would be Dominick. Dom attended our school from the time he was five until he was fourteen. He was a child who loved to play, be outside, talk, draw, and build. We knew early on, when he was five and six, that he had trouble learning how to read and write. He worked with Rhea, who was quoted in the introduction, every day when he was seven and eight. He had a leadership year, which is having a teacher for a second year , in every group until his was eleven.

During high school he did well, but it wasn't until he was going to Oakland University that an advisor told him that he was dyslexic. Dom knew what that meant, but before he could speak the advisor said, "I've never met anyone like you. You're so skilled verbally, and you've developed skills to do all of the reading at this level, but what impresses me most about you is your confidence. There's no quit in you and no hint of self-deprecation."

Dominick graduated from Oakland University and had a successful career in the corporate world. He and his wife enrolled their daughter in our school and just last year he was hired to teach the oldest morning-meeting group.

He reports that this is the steepest learning curve he's ever experienced. He loves teaching, and following Ted he has a clear challenge ahead of him. Those leadership years when he was a student are as evident to us as they were to his university advisor. He told me recently that he didn't like going to Rhea at first, but he knew we loved him, and he had developed a trust in us that felt to him more like the trust of an uncle or an aunt. So even though he wanted to play outside with his friends, he went to Rhea, and she helped him develop the strategies that he's using today. And he grew into a man with self-confidence, kindness, community values, and multiple skills.

Buckminster Fuller said "every child is a genius," and Krishnamurti talked about the necessity of learning about our inner self. Both adopted grandfathers pointed me in the direction of looking for the genius in each child and discovering the vast inner universe of ourselves. This was a form of rewiring. I needed proof that every child was a genius, so I began to look for their gift, and it was not difficult at all. I noticed very quickly how each child brought something unique to the entire school and began looking for a way to support it and communicate it.

When I discovered Howard Gardner's book *Frames of Mind*, it was like reading an answer to my prayers. Here was a theory of "multiple intelligences," and it fit so beautifully with both Bucky's and K's ideas. It was in the early eighties that we began to first integrate this into our curriculum, and until just recently I thought that was when we first began using the ideas of Howard Gardner.

In the course of researching an innovative holistic curriculum we began using in the mid-seventies called "Man: A Course of Study," I discovered that one of the young researchers for this amazing, leading-edge set of films, short books, games, songs, and poetry was none other than Howard Gardner. The big question in "Man: A Course of Study," which we now refer to as "Human: A Course of Study," was, "What is human about human beings?"

In chapter four we will explore how the theory of multiple intelligences can be applied to every child and used by every teacher to improve the future of children. By looking at the breadth and scope of all human intelligences—not just the ones measured by IQ tests—we will discover some possible answers to Jerome Bruner's big question, "What is human about human beings?"

Chapter Four

GARDNER'S CHILDREN

We need to teach the next generation of children from day one that they are responsible for their lives. Mankind's greatest gift, also its greatest curse, is that we have free choice. We can make our choices built from love or from fear.

—*Elisabeth Kübler-Ross, guest teacher at Upland Hills School, 1993*

A few years after we completed Project School House, our Upland Hills Ecological Awareness Center hosted a paradigm-shifter named Elisabeth Kübler-Ross. Elisabeth's book *On Death and Dying*, first published a few years before our school was founded, transformed the perception of death in our postmodern world. Today's hospice movement was deeply inspired by her work and her wisdom.

Her talk to our community was held in the big room of our new schoolhouse. During her question-and-answer period, someone asked her, "What gives you hope?" She paused for a moment and looked around the room and answered, "Being here in a school like this." As we were saying goodbye to each other, she told me that being in the school surrounded by the children's art, poetry, articles of clothing, wood-working projects, and clay bowls touched her heart. When I began to write out a check for her travel-and-speaking fee, she asked if she could make a donation to our school. After donating her entire speaking fee and taking only plane fare, she said that she could feel how alive our school was and that the natural world was not only present, it was the essence of that aliveness. "You're not just teaching the three R's here," she said. "Something else has taken their place."

That something else was applying Howard Gardner's theory of multiple intelligences on a daily basis and experiencing how lines of intelligence intertwine and co-emerge. The other part of that something else was that our school was determined to do just what Elisabeth said. We were determined to teach children that they are responsible for their lives and that they need to learn how to make choices. A love-based environment can inform those choices and let them learn from their direct experiences about the differences between a love-based and a fear-based choice.

What's My Line?

There was a television game show that ran from 1950 until 1967 called *What's My Line?* The four panelists would try to determine who the contestant was by asking questions that could be answered with a simple "yes" or "no." This hugely popular game show has something in common with Howard Gardner's theory of multiple intelligences.

When a prospective student comes to our school for a visit day, every staff member is like a panel member of *What's My Line?* Our teachers, along with the child's parents, share an essential curiosity very similar to the seasoned panelists on that show. We too are listening for and looking for clues to discover what line or lines of intelligence this child has a passion for. Sometimes we discover it very quickly; sometimes it changes as the child develops; and sometimes it emerges suddenly as if it were waiting for just the right set of conditions.

The lines of intelligence that Gardner identified are: bodily-kinesthetic, logical-mathematical, verbal-linguistic, visual-spatial, musical, intrapersonal, interpersonal, natural, and existential. We all have multiple intelligences. We are on the lookout for one particular area of intelligence where the child shows considerable interest and capabilities. When Willie showed up at our school with his child-sized accordion and began composing songs as a five-year-old, we knew that music had already cast it's spell of enchantment on him. (You will read more about Willie shortly.)

The huge difference between thinking of the brain as one central, all-purpose computer and thinking of our brain as having a number of relatively autonomous computers is the central brilliance of Gardner's theory.

Bodily-Kinesthetic: Kacey at the Bat

By the time Kacey joined our school as a seven-year-old, she knew that she loved to compete. Her dad was a physical education teacher in a local public school, and Kacey had inherited his love for playing hard and playing to win. She took to our school like a hawk to the air. She loved her teacher, who had developed a curriculum that included at least two outdoor breaks every morning and who always wanted to play with his kids during those breaks.

Her favorite time of the day was immediately following lunch. She'd bolt out of the classroom as soon as she finished eating and stand in the center of the field to be picked for that day's game. It didn't matter what game was being played. It didn't even cross her mind that often she was the only girl on the field. It didn't matter that she was on the younger end of the spectrum, and it didn't matter how physical or rough the game was. What did matter was that there would be teams and that one team would win and the other lose, and that she could totally lose herself in the flow of that game.

Whether it was soccer or football, capture the flag or baseball, Kacey was playing her heart out and happy to be free. By the time she was ten she had established herself as a team leader, with exceptional skills and a heart that had no quit in it. The older boys who played with similar intensity respected her, and more than one developed a crush on her. She was oblivious to it all. What she did care about was rallying her team to not give up. She learned how to inspire the moody boys who were already complaining before the game even started, and she learned how to keep her team focused and alert.

By the time she was eleven and twelve she was leading the games. Kacey was often the captain of the team and more often than not the person who made the touchdown catch, or scored the final goal, or assisted on the double play, or attempted the diving catch in the mud. She modeled true sportsmanship or, more accurately, she modeled true sportswomanship. When her team lost, she would congratulate the winning team and thank her teammates for playing so hard. Her first teacher, David, used to report in staff meetings that when Kacey was on the field there was no need for a teacher to be refereeing the game. She had earned the respect of every child on and off the field.

When Kacey left our school, she attended a public middle school and a public high school. As an adult she now knows that even before she came to our school she felt like she was being caged in. She saw the fences around her school's playground and instead of feeling safe, she felt hemmed in. While she was at our school, she felt free in a way that was more like her own country home. During middle school and high school, she participated in school sports like volleyball and soccer, but that closed-in feeling came up while in class. She discovered in high school that she always had a difficult time concentrating if she had to sit for long periods of time. She realized that the reason she did so well at our school was because of all the opportunities she had to run free.

When Kacey turned eighteen, she discovered bicycle racing. This led to a scholarship in North Carolina and eventually a move to Pennsylvania to be closer to the T-Town velodrome track. Her bicycle training and racing led to international travel and to the highest levels of that sport. Yet it was something totally unexpected in 2008 that led to one of the peak experiences of her life as an athlete.

Because she had offered a ride to a friend in North Carolina to New York City, she ended up entering the first Red Hook Crit. This event started in Brooklyn in 2008 as an unsanctioned fixed-bike (no brakes) night race. Kacey, whose motto among bike enthusiasts is "Find your passion, Take Chances," set out to just finish the race and hold her own against a male-dominant field. But after dodging traffic, taking 180 degree turns without brakes, and experiencing her 100% commitment to winning, she developed a strategy on the home stretch and won the race.

The race now occurs on both sides of the Atlantic and attracts thousands of fans. Kacey is an organizer and leader of this event and considered an icon. She's the girl that surprised everybody. The girl who won the first Red Hook Crit.

The woman who won the first Red Hook Crit has come to a few conclusions about her life as an athlete. The first one is that there is something selfish about devoting so much time and effort to sport. She plans to use her skills to help nonprofits thrive. The second conclusion is that because of bicycle racing she has been given a gift beyond any win. That gift is the gift of worldwide friendship. Wherever she travels there are bicycle enthusiasts who eagerly put her up. The third conclusion has to do with something she experienced in her last corporate job. While sitting in her skyscraper office building, she had this flash that this too was a cage. She is determined to live her life outside of any cage and to raise her children with a love for being outside.

One of Kacey's lines of intelligence is the bodily-kinesthetic line. This line that she developed and pursued has led her to her husband, to her home in Pennsylvania, her insight about freedom, her community, and her life as a leader. Yes, we could say that this is her primary line, but as she was developing this line, the lines of interpersonal intelligence and intrapersonal intelligence were also developing.

While her father was undergoing treatment for prostate cancer, her mother told him that they would be taking a surprise field trip after the treatment. He didn't have the energy to resist her, but he knew that he didn't really want to be with people. She drove him directly from the hospital to our school, and he knew as soon as they turned north and east where she was taking him.

They got out of the car and walked around the school, remembering their two daughters playing and laughing, growing into the two amazing women they would become. They walked arm in arm, and we embraced at the end of the school's bridge. Ed's eyes were full of tears, yet his smile was present. Both of his children loved to play and loved to win, just like their father, but they also knew that there was much more to life than winning. There were camping trips into the wild. There was Isle Royal National Park, and there was the delight of living free from the boundaries of convention. Kacey's mom and dad gave their girls something precious, something beyond pursuing a win. They gave their girls the support and encouragement to be true to their essential selves. How proud he would be to hear his daughter say, "I believe in doing things you love and have passion for—your work and effort are always better when you have passion behind them. Taking chances is part of the game. If you always play it safe, you'll never realize your full potential in anything."

Musical Intelligence: Willie Writes a Song

When Willie was five years old, he wrote the lyrics for a song. He owned a children's accordion and played it whenever he felt happy, which was quite often. He came to me and asked if I would write the music for his song. With the help of his teacher, Jean, they had written the lyrics out:

> *Upland Hills is a great place to be*
> *It's loaded with fun and lots of joy*
> *The teachers are nice, mine is Jean*
> *I wish I could go there forever*
> *But forever is too good to be true*
> *So I guess I'll go to high school*
> *When I'm finished*

I took out my banjo and noodled around for a bit while Will smiled on. We sang together and found a simple C-F-G progression that seemed to work. We laughed when it all fell into place, and just like that a new song was born.

Music plays an integral role in our school culture. From the very first year of our school, every all-school-meeting has begun with a few songs. Four decades later we have an entire song repertoire that is continually evolving. Before the seventies were out, we instituted a mandatory music class for every group that is still in place today. We discovered the genius of Carl Orff, a German composer who used a five-note (pentatonic) scale to teach children to play in an open-ended improvisational style. His teaching methods, which were spread through the American Orff-Schulwerk Association based in Indiana, found their way to our school through a retired music teacher named Joe. Joe became my mentor for an entire year, and watching him work with children was a revelation. Joe would set up the dome classroom with fifteen instruments set for the five-note scale; the children would come in, sit down, and play beautiful music.

By the time Willie joined our school community we were working with developmental music pieces based on the Orff-Schulwerk method for the first three groups. He and his classmates learned from the earliest ages how to play together and how to improvise off of a musical theme. The older three groups learned how to read music and how to blend their favorite instruments into carefully chosen songs, some of which were written by our own Ted Strunck.

Our school community is mystically based on this one line of intelligence. We discovered how transcendent it was to sing beautifully crafted lyrics with melodies that connected beyond our logical minds. From the traditional Canadian folk song "Land of the Silver Birch" to India Arie's "I am Light," our school culture is continually infused with a wide variety of musical styles and genres. But the one person who inspired Willie the most was one of our global faculty members: Eugene Friesen.

Eugene and I met through the celebrated saxophonist Paul Winter. Our Upland Hills Ecological Awareness Center hosted the Paul Winter Consort with his special guest Yevgeny Yevtushenko, the Russian poet, for an event called "A Concert for the Earth." While Eugene and I were editing a video from that concert, we discussed the idea of a cello program for children. By the time Willie was attending our school, Eugene was our guest teacher nearly every year. His program was called "Cello Man," and one particular student was so struck with the beauty of that instrument and the "wild" way it could be used in improvisation that he decided to take it on as his own.

Willie's first calling to the cello was when he heard a recording of Yo-Yo Ma's Bach cello suites, but it was "Cello Man" who sealed the deal. Willie listened in rapt attention to Eugene's "Cello Man." From an improvisation on the Hungarian composer Béla Bartók's theme, a composition he called "Dances with Rasputin," to a duet with a blue whale, Willie was enchanted. While the audience was laughing with delight as Cello Man put on a squirrel mask and played his cello the way a squirrel might, Willie must have been dreaming about cello for dessert. Eugene closed his "Cello Man" concert by transforming into Pablo Casals as he untangles his arthritic ninety-five-year-old fingers and comes back to life by playing a Bach cello solo. The sounds of the cello hang in the air as the final notes are played, and Pablo collapses back into old age.

That is how Will Rowe came to be a cello player and composer. Perhaps I should say that this is how Will Rowe became the assistant director of the New Music Ensemble at Indiana University, or this is how Will Rowe came to win the BMI Student Composer Award, or how he came to perform for the 2013 ISCM World New Music Days Festival in Vienna, Austria, but in reality one never knows how such things happen. Eugene has performed "Cello Man" in front of hundreds of Upland Hills School students, and only one of them has taken up cello and stayed with it into adulthood.

Willie also fell in love with the natural world at our school and has woven that love into his music. He cares deeply about issues like climate change and knows from direct experience that the wind and the sun can produce energy without dumping more carbon dioxide into our atmosphere. He seeks out close intimate friendships and especially cherishes his Upland Hills friends. His friendship with Eugene is unique because it began when he first discovered his love for music and particularly for the cello. He practiced hard to get to the moment when the two of them performed a cello duet, and it was during their rehearsal that Willie had the opportunity to talk cello to cello with a master of improvisation.

Music as a line of intelligence deserves a place in the pantheon of what new-paradigm schools should teach. We often see how music is thought of as the class we first cut when our public schools need to save money, but in the new paradigm we will come to see it the other way around. Music is the very essence of the new paradigm because it inspires, unites, and integrates like nothing else.

Interpersonal Intelligence: Kelley Climbs a Mountain

Kelley came to our school ready to relate. He is the youngest child in a blended family of educators. His father was a professor of education at Wayne State University who was deeply admired for his strong stance on human rights and responsibilities. His mother was an advocate for creativity and self-authoring who, as a school principal, led her school with dignity and daring. He has three older siblings who were more like parents because of the significant age difference between them and him. And each of them had lifelong distinguished carriers in education.

Kelley's gift is in his ability to relate to people of all ages. He loves to interact with others, and he is a skillful communicator who listens deeply and uses a nuanced vocabulary. Kelley has the ability to read people quickly and to understand their motives and feelings.

The challenge from the moment I met his parents and from his very first day at our school, and for the next eight years, was that Kelley was not a student. Let me explain. Kelley loved everything about school except for schoolwork. He quickly understood the game of school and thrived in many areas. Give him a lead role in a musical, or give him a movie camera and a crew, and he was off creating. Watch him begin a pick-up touch football game, and you'd see a born leader. But in a classroom setting where there were reading and writing assignments, tests or quizzes, memorization of facts rather than lines, he just checked out. He did this checking out in the most creative and endearing way.

I was his teacher for his last two years at our school, which we call the transition years, essentially seventh and eighth grades. It was my imagined job to help prepare Kelley for a public high school. When it came time for a report to be due, there would be not a report, only a long conversation. When it came time for a test, there would be a poor grade and then another long conversation. When it came time for math, there would be ever-lengthening trips to the bathroom inversely proportional to learning how to factor quadratic equations.

I spoke with his parents at the end of each trimester, when they listened carefully and then invited the entire staff for a Christmas dinner. In short Kelley confounded me, and I worried that I had not prepared him for high school. But what I failed to understand at that time was how his ability to interact with a wide range of people, coupled with his understanding of himself, would be the essential ingredients he would need to navigate his life in Earth School.

The mystical edge of being a teacher has to do with the huge domain of "what you don't know you don't know." As we learn and grow, we come to understand that "what we know we know" is an infinitesimally small domain. What we know we don't know is somewhat bigger, but the biggest one of all is what we don't know we don't know.

What I didn't know about Kelley was that during those long, heart-to-heart talks we'd have about the missing home-work assignments we were forming an unbreakable bond that transcended our roles. Kelley had understood that his father's old age meant that he would not have his father in his life for as long as he wanted it. He had adopted me as a second father. When I went to India to find my essential self, he would take a similar trip years later. When I went to Maine to experience the wild that my mentor Buckminster Fuller loved so much, he would follow and live there for a time. When his father died, he would call and ask me if I would lead the service, and when his mother died, he and his sisters would make the same request.

When he married, Karen and I not only happily attended, but we were also invited to share a portion of their honeymoon with them. We have prayed together in sweat lodges, walked the streets of Chicago sharing intimate stories about our lives, and we have continued to deepen our love for the mystery that brought us together.

The mountain that Kelley had to climb was not unlike the mountains his father had to climb during World War II when he was rescuing his band of brothers in the Po Valley. It was a mountain of creative educators who had all graduated from universities with advanced degrees and made their mark in their respective fields. Kelley had to navigate a different set of circumstances that often left him alone in his rural Oxford, Michigan, home. He had to use his gift of interpersonal intelligence to discover how to provide for his two children in a complex world without a degree from a university. He earned his degree through his adventures, his mistakes, his insights about life and death, his career as a singer-songwriter, and his willingness to take risks.

His father wrote, "Responsibility cannot be learned in the absence of freedom; nor can respect for law and order be learned in the absence of respecting experience. Teachers must be freed from school and classroom practices which demean, diminish, and/or destroy a child's feelings of self-worth."

His youngest son would live his life free from ever being diminished in school, at least in his formative years. That did not, however, mean that he would never diminish himself or have to wrestle the demons of self-loathing. Perhaps because he knew intuitively that he was loved deeply and encouraged to develop his line of interpersonal intelligence that he succeeded in becoming a real-estate agent in Chicago. One thing for sure is that he is people smart.

Intrapersonal Intelligence: A Rose that's Always in Bloom

Marcia Rose was one of the founders of Upland Hills Farm School. While Karen, Nina, and I were exploring Europe and North Africa from the fall of 1970 until the fall of 1971, Marcia and her former husband were meeting together with the founders of Upland Hills Farm to create a school. A small group of parents and educators came together to create a place for their children that would be creative, relevant, and diverse. This group laid the foundation for the school that we would first visit in October of 1971.

It included a professor of children's literature from Wayne State University, Tom Hamil, who had three children and would become the school's first director. It also included Knight and Dorothy Webster, the founders of Upland Hills Farm and whose youngest child would be among the first students, and Marcia and Chuck Loznak, who had three children. Marcia Rose would play an integral role as a guiding parent, teacher, and program director of Upland Hills Ecological Awareness Center, until her children graduated from our school and she eventually moved to Barre, Massachusetts.

She moved to Barre to become a resident teacher for the staff at the Insight Meditation Society from 1991 until 1995. Marcia began practicing meditation in 1970, and as her practice deepened so did her calling to devote her life to guiding and maintaining the Mountain Hermitage of Taos, New Mexico. This is where she lives today teaching meditation retreats that range from a few days to five weeks.

Meditation is to intrapersonal intelligence as water is to life. When we met, Marcia was first and foremost a mother who was determined to raise her children in a creative and loving environment. We became good friends very quickly, and I watched her as she met one challenge after another. I worked very closely by her side for twenty years and over that time watched her navigate a divorce, the sudden loss of a job, the raising of two demanding children and one introspective child, career changes, money problems, and a house fire that destroyed most of her possessions.

At her root there was always meditation. She recently wrote this:

Everything has its season. Everything arises and passes away ... endlessly. The end of anything always provides space for the beginning of something else ... the seasons and my garden teaching this to me every year. The tiny moments of our lives hold this same teaching as the experience of each moment gives way to the experience of the next moment. If we try to hold on to summer or any moment that we're in, the heart contracts. We feel pain.

There is an almost invisible apex that manifests at the end and the beginning of seasons and moments. It is at this subtle point in the ceaseless changing nature of things where the innate manifestation of creativity lies. The garden naturally knows this and never tries to hold back, cling on or resist. I'm still learning and am so grateful for my living breathing teacher, my garden.

Intrapersonal intelligence at the level that Marcia has attained deeply affects the people around her, and her work has helped develop the growing interest in living spiritual lives centered in mindfulness and loving-kindness. Thich Nhat Hanh, the Buddhist teacher and author, has said that the next Buddha will be a sangha or community. Perhaps this is why she has always been interested in forming and living in communities. The practice of meditation is the ability to be aware and awake in the present moment. While Marcia was a teacher at our school, she taught dance and movement as well as Women's Class. Her direction at that time was to empower young girls to be able to change a tire, dance with joy, bond deeply with the natural world, and to leave our campsite (and the world) better than we found it.

When she became a massage therapist, she used her skills to relieve, restore, and heal. She helped to build our Ecological Awareness Center by becoming a fine stonemason and, after it was completed, its program director. We worked together to offer programs that explored meditation, alternative healing, transformational music, leading-edge teachers, and alternative energy sources.

For the past thirteen years she and her community members have pulled off a miracle in this day and age. Together they have maintained a nonprofit organization dedicated to extended retreats so that people from all walks of life can deepen their practice and insight.

In a recent article at the Mountain Hermitage website, she writes:

The active force of a peaceful, lucid and undisturbed state of mind attained by the practice of strong mental concentration begins by gathering together the potentially powerful energy of the mind that ordinarily is quite dispersed. The initial act of concentration reins the mind in from its myriad distractions. We then learn how to focus it by coming back again and again to the simple present so that our mental and physical energy isn't being used up or usurped in unconscious and unskillful ways. For this, one needs a willingness rooted in the wholesome intention to stay present with the chosen object of attention, along with the development of clearly knowing when the attention gets lost in something other than what is intended. A clear, relaxed and focused mind feeds itself as our ability to stay present with the object of attention and not attach to other things strengthens. The mind is just where it is . . . pure, clear, and calm . . . which can be an energizing, refreshing and beautiful experience.

Marcia Rose changed my life. She taught me by example. The years we worked together were years of continual learning and stretching. The ease I felt in her presence helped me to surrender into a focused energy field that serves something beyond ourselves. The inner subjective world of intrapersonal intelligence is the source for true teaching. When children and adults are in the presence of someone who is openhearted, compassionate, and available, they too open into the flowers of their higher selves. This is why Marcia is much like her chosen name, for she is like a rose that is always in bloom.

Verbal Linguistic:
Laughter, Language & Leslie

*A famous celebrity has twins at age 40. Four months later
we see her in a bikini on the cover of a magazine: How
Jennifer Got Back Her Pre-Pregnancy Body. Meanwhile
our hair is dirty, we're wearing a stained sweatshirt, and
the waist band on our pants is still feeling awfully tight.*

—*Leslie Irish Evans,*
from Peeling Mom Off the Ceiling

Leslie attended our school for three years. When she was about eleven years old, she introduced herself as coming from a blended family: "Kind of like the Brady Bunch, but we don't have as much fun." She was smart, observant, engaging, and funny. I was her teacher for her last two years, and although we shared some very sad and difficult moments, I can't think of her without smiling.

Leslie seemed to know what she had while she was having it. How rare that is. She had already experienced traditional public school, so she knew from day one that she was not in Kansas anymore. She also knew that the freedom and the informality were only a part of what she was experiencing. During an interview for a documentary film we were making at the time, she observed that, "Upland Hills School is a place where you can be who you were meant to be." In many ways I believe she would have flourished wherever she attended school, but something special happened at our school that turned an already "on" person into a super nova.

That something was the theatre. It was when she made an entrance as Captain Hook that we all took notice. She was transformed, alive, and brilliant, as she fully inhabited that snide nemesis of Peter Pan. Like all great actors she spoke her lines from inside of the character, and even though the audience was only nine inches away we were all convinced that the cunning captain was prowling our deck. It was also true that she was the real Alice in wonderland and the one and only Little Orphan Annie.

She sang, she strutted, she bellowed, and she cried, and we were all enchanted. During our group time and in the afternoon classes, Leslie was so fully engaged it was as if she, her mom, and her new stepfather had given her the greatest gift ever. It was the gift of a school that loved the arts. She was a great writer, a book lover, a filmmaker, a stand-up comic, and a people person.

All human beings possess all nine intelligences in varying degrees, and Leslie was and is strong in several of them, but the line of verbal-linguistic intelligence sticks out for this reason: she can use words that make you laugh. There is something about humor that defies any rational explanation. Why is funny impossible to teach? How is it that comedy can sometimes reveal more about our pain than tragedy? How come the Dali Lama, who loves laughter, can't tell a joke?

In class Leslie was always able to state her point of view with clarity and insight. But the thing that I remember most about having her as my student is the laughter.

At the end of our school year, Karen offers a talent show where any child from any group can offer something up as entertainment. These sometimes long, drawn-out, rehearsed-once performances often present us with the talking chins, the skit that has no end and no point, or the "Here's a chance to throw a pie in someone's face" acts. But forever imprinted in my mind was the day when Leslie and her best friend Kristi opened the door to our portable classroom and entered with their version of Saturday Night Live's "Two Wild and Crazy

Guys." There's Leslie dressed as a wild and crazy Czech sister announcing the new Miss America, and in walks Kristi shaking and moving like a true wild and crazy Czech sister.

The entire staff is still in recovery.

Her book *Peeling Mom off the Ceiling* is pure Leslie. It's a personal yet universal story of how to use humor to find yourself once you've lost yourself down the rabbit hole of mothering. Her book is a perfect companion to Dr. Shefali's *The Conscious Parent* in that both books are asking us to discover deep spiritual insights through the raising of our children. Leslie was with us for three years, essentially her seventh through ninth grades. When she came to us, she already had a foundation beyond her years for the line of language. However, during her public school experience she was often the teacher's pet and allowed to work apart from the class because she was the smart kid the teacher didn't have to worry about. The line of intelligence that Leslie clearly displayed when she attended our school has been nurtured, developed, supported, and enhanced so that mothers all over this world —and let's face it, fathers too—can come to appreciate the almost impossible task of childrearing in the twenty-first century.

She writes, "My kids were born 21 months apart. I don't remember much of anything between 1993 and 1996, to be honest. I've seen pictures, though. I look tired."

When Leslie came back to school for a concert honoring my forty-two-year run, the first thing she did was offer me a copy of her book. The synchronicity of it was that I had often thought of her helping me write a book, and now in some mysterious way she is. We had only a moment during that evening but enough time to be with her mom and her mother's new boyfriend. Leslie had traveled from Seattle to Detroit for this visit. Her presence that evening reminded me of how fast it had all gone. How did 1980 turn into 2013?

I now know that I will always be grateful to have been Leslie's teacher, and I will always be indebted to her. She brought a synergistic ingredient to our school that increased the levity and the laughty of each moment. And she did it all with words and great timing. She recently said:

> Upland Hills School met me where I was and saw the potential of what was inside me. Rather than set me aside and say, 'Oh she's a smart girl. There are others that need to be brought up to speed,' they found my fuse and lit it, saying, 'Let's see how high this kid can fly!' "

Logical-Mathematical: Shaun's Magic, Mushrooms & Mathematics

I first met Shaun when he was five years old. His curly hair made me think of Albert Einstein at that age. His smile was infectious and so was his enthusiasm for learning. He loved everything about school. He loved being a part of a community. He loved being outdoors. He loved his friends. He loved being at school with his older brother, and he loved being alive.

I taught an afternoon class called Wild Foods, and little Shaun went to our class every time it was offered until he became big Shaun. For nine years he would follow me as we harvested the first bracken ferns of the season, found a stand of wild asparagus, discovered how to use the tubers of the cattail, and drank sumac lemonade. By the time he was ten he had discovered a few wild places at school and near his home where the coveted morel mushroom could be found. This was the gold of wild foods, and Shaun and I both knew that he had surpassed me as the "wild guru of wild foods." I was humbled and delighted because unlike some Wild Foods class members,

Shaun loved to share his bounty with others, and he would always save me the largest white morel.

I was also Shaun's math teacher. I taught the oldest kids at school, which meant that I was teaching Algebra I and II, as well as Synergetic Geometry, Buckminster Fuller's geometry based on nature's design instead of platonic structures that were entirely theoretical (planes and solids). I had also taught his older brother Brett, who transcended me in advanced algebra the way Shaun had transcended me as a mushroom hunter. I remember coming home after a day of teaching Brett something complex like matrix algebra and needing to spend a few hours learning what I eventually knew would take ten minutes for Brett to understand. It was not a sustainable relationship.

As Shaun's math teacher I decided to use our time to explore mathematics and logic as a line of intelligence that offered opportunities to learn how to think and how to construct models. This allowed us to learn together and to explore the geometry of thinking with a small group of kids who had the ability to absorb and understand ideas and integrities far quicker than their teacher. I decided to fire myself as the math teacher for the older group at the end of that year.

Teaching kids like Shaun and Brett math is like teaching an ocean lover how to surf. All you have to do is get them to the top of a wave and let them find its power. They both dove into the books and concepts with excitement and agility. My job was to keep them inspired and interested. Witnessing them move beyond my knowledge base was like having an out-of-body experience. I was no longer the little me. I was somehow in them, and they were moving so fast that I felt like the rocket booster that was required to break gravity and not needed once that was accomplished.

Shaun graduated from the University of Colorado fifth in his class, majoring in physics and receiving many honors and a scholarship along the way. We hired him to teach at our school for five years. He taught Advanced Math, Wild Foods, Men's Class, Carpentry, and the Adventure Playground (a ropes course). It moves my heart to tears thinking about Shaun as a five-year-old, as a teacher, and as our adopted son.

When our school was searching for the new director, Shaun applied and at twenty-eight years old was almost selected as the next director.

I visited Shaun when he was living on Maui and I was looking for a place to write during the winter. During our time together, he took me on adventures that he thought I would love. Every Shaun trip was a gem. One of them was a drive to a hidden trail. When we got to the trail, we hiked up a mountain on narrow paths that were rigged with ropes and handmade signs. All I knew was that we were going to a waterfall. When we finally arrived, we dove into one of three small pools of clear mountain water. We swam for a time, and then Shaun motioned for me to come over to the edge.

Very slowly I made my way to the rock where Shaun was balancing on. He walked from one side of the falls to the other. My heart was in my throat. There were no fences, no warnings, no signs. I looked over the last rock and saw the water that was in our pools falling over two hundred feet into a deep pool far, far below. Shaun was balanced beyond where I would ever want to go. I looked at him as he looked beyond the edge and took in a magnificent view. I wanted to pull an imaginary rope around his waist and bring him back into the swimming pool, but I wasn't his father. I was his guest, and he was my guide. I watched him stay there for a time and then lie down on the very edge of the top of the waterfall and rest with a huge smile on his face. How could he be so at ease and I so fearful?

I dove back into the pool with its clear edges and shallow bottom and tried to let go of the worry and thoughts in my mind. I heard him enter the pool, and we swam together without words and without any concern for time. His line of mathematics and logic, which he cultivated to its higher levels, was also entwined with his line of naturalist intelligence and to his lines of inter- and intrapersonal intelligence. His exploration and skill that he had already obtained were now a coherent, interwoven set that enabled him to travel, inquire, and delve into his life's purpose without being constrained by scarcity. Both he and his brother have learned enough about the world and how money works to live lives that open up time and provide opportunities to pursue the big questions in life. How do we find true happiness? What does right livelihood look like for me? How do we find, form, or develop authentic community? How do we evolve the current paradigm into the next one? They have done this by utilizing their ability to think and problem-solve. In short they have done this by using high levels of mathematics/logic and applying it to paying their bills while maintaining their freedom.

For Shaun, his ability to form his own DJ business, coupled with a lifelong practice of saving money and doing more with less, has enabled him to maintain a high quality of life. He also is deeply connected to his friends and family and is always expanding both of those domains. Brett has used his childhood love of the game Magic to buy and sell cards over the Internet with a combination of skill and ethics that would make the heroes of *The Big Short* take notice.

They both are currently sharing a house in Boulder, Colorado. They both have dreams and the skills to match. Perhaps they are the new wave of social artists who want to find ways to protect the systems and beauty of the natural world, while also discovering the new-paradigm ways of living a life of meaning that honors all sentient beings. They may be among the leaders on the cutting edge of a transformed, sustainable, interconnected world where everyone on the planet matters.

Visual-Spatial Intelligence: Let's Play, Tim Damon!

Tim's mother put on her lace gloves, her high-heeled shoes, and her perfectly chosen dress to make the best impression during her first interview with our school. She got a bit confused about the connection between Upland Hills Farm and Upland Hills School and ended up stuck in a morass of mud between the two. Frustrated, late, and flustered she opened the car door, stepped into the mud, and followed a path that had an old sign with a point that simply read "school."

When she arrived she looked like she had crossed the wilderness that divided the future from the past. She asked for the powder room, and I guided her to one of the two bathrooms in our portable classrooms, the one that didn't have the chicken in it. She came out a bit more composed and started talking to me about her son. It was a familiar story. A boy who was lost in public school, was placed in a special-education room, had trouble reading and writing, was very unhappy, and hated going to school.

Tim transformed by the end of his first week of attending our school. He had gone from that unhappy boy to being one of the most alive, vibrant, creative, engaging, irrepressible, and engaged students we had ever experienced. He made friends very quickly and was thrilled by the number of choices we offered in the afternoons. He was excited about everything that moved. Aviation class, rockets, filmmaking, and theatre play-shop were among his favorite classes—but it wasn't just the classes. It wasn't just the fact that he could choose to be outdoors so much or the quality or variety of kids we had; it was the contrast between prison and freedom.

Tim loved movie making. He loved new technology, and he loved combining speed and light with pictures. It didn't matter whether it was a still or a motion picture; it was the magic of the lens and how it interacted with shadow and light that fascinated Tim. As his interest in pictures grew, so did his confidence in himself. He developed strategies to memorize lines and to read for information by relying on pictures and diagrams. He began to experience life as a series of roadblocks that he needed to learn how to navigate around. Tim learned by doing things, by experimenting with how things work, and by forming a close friendship with a boy who was terminally ill.

Ted and Tim bonded quickly. They both knew that they had no time to waste and that too much time had already been wasted. Ted was an only child who had been born into a well-to-do family, but because of his dyslexia he had been forced to do the thing he had come to hate the most, which was learning how to read. When Ted was diagnosed as having a severe form of childhood leukemia, it was a turning point for him and for his family. The priorities got turned upside down. Reading fell to the bottom of their list (it was already on the bottom of Ted's), and happiness went straight to the top, which fit perfectly with who Ted was.

The two boys formed a pact. They would attempt to live life at the speed of light. They would sleep over at each other's houses as much as possible. They would sled until darkness every day there was snow. They would break any rule that forbid them to be together, and they would invent ways to remember each other that left some scars but, like a brand, would last forever.

By the time that Ted died, Tim had already been deeply imprinted. Tim not only watched his best friend fight cancer, come back from each chemotherapy determined to win, and through his illness bring his quarreling family together, he experienced it all as if it were happening to him. All of this before Tim reached fourteen years of age.

Tim graduated from our school and received special auditory assistance in his private Catholic high school. He attended the College for Creative Studies in Detroit, but nothing could explain how he decided one day to leave Detroit for Los Angeles with no plan, no money, no place to stay, and only a dream about how to capture light in pictures and on film.

I arrived in LA fifteen years ago on a fund-raising mission for our school. Tim had asked me not to rent a car or arrange for anyone to pick me up; he wanted to handle those things. I was met at LAX by one of his employees, who drove me to Long Beach where Tim's offices were at the time. When I arrived Tim greeted me warmly, and as soon as we went into his office I noticed the TV screens were on, and somehow Tim was tuned into the world as much as he was tuned into me. He took me into what looked like an airplane hangar and invited me to choose any one of his cars for the week I would be in town.

He was running his own company and had surrounded himself with a team of smart, experienced, talented, and crazy warriors. I marveled at the number of projects and innovations he was working on, and it wasn't until we had some time together that I got to hear one of his unforgettable stories.

It was about being late for a meeting, driving in South Korea, with his Harvard-educated assistant navigating. They were approaching their exit when they noticed it was closed. Tim passed it, and his assistant yelled at his boss, "What are you doing?'" "I'm doing what I've done my entire life, navigating around road blocks." They were just ten minutes late to their meeting, and they got the business.

Tim is still operating his own business. Last time we saw each other he shared his excitement about his Lexus commercial for the 2015 Super Bowl. Tim is one of Hollywood's most highly regarded car-commercial directors. He also owns and operates two other companies, a production company and a fully integrated camera-car-system company, designing ways to capture speed and light on film.

Tim's visual-spatial intelligence, his interpersonal skills, his drive, and his creativity have taken him to the top of one of the most competitive and complex fields in our global marketplace. He brings an unusual amount of energy and skill to every project. He wants to do great work and is not willing to settle for anything less. While talking as we walked along the oceanfront on Venice Beach, he showed me the scar on his arm from the cat that Ted threw at him. His mark. We spoke about Ted's last days, and for those moments it seemed as if Ted was alive. "He was crazy you know," Tim said.

His eyes filled with tears remembering his best friend. I thought of the courage and willingness that it took for Tim to leave home. I thought of the courage and the willingness it took to recover from a crushed dream when Tim blew out his ACL and could no longer compete as a downhill skier. I thought of the courage and willingness it takes to keep reinventing not only yourself, but your business in Hollywood. Then I remembered that scar from Ted's cat and thought to myself maybe Tim is living two lives instead of one.

The Naturalist:
Dylan, the Smiling Runner
of White Mountain

A line of intelligence that Howard Gardner added to the original seven is called the "naturalist." People who are drawn to this line of intelligence are those who love to be out under the sky. We lean into the natural world to learn and to be healed, to discover how the world outside connects to our world inside. This line of intelligence when summarized by the psychologists means "understanding living things and reading nature." At our school we say it this way: The natural world is our primary teacher.

Dylan came to us a shy seven-year-old who was being raised by a strong single mother. She lived within walking distance of our school in a house that was rented by a group of people who were attracted to the school and to the farm. This communal household was her new family. The bedrooms were full and so was the energy of the house. This fullness was the context for her to have many parents, as well as an adopted sister and brother. She loved it.

The three Upland Hills students would get up each morning, pack their lunches, and set off to school. The primary adult-approved route was a trail that led directly from their back door through a few neighbors' ten-acre lots and out to a driveway that placed them directly across from the school's driveway. It was a scenic, hilly route that avoided Indian Lake Road, a tree-lined country road that had a little bit of traffic just before and just after school began and let out. The kids eventually realized that if they took a beeline to Indian Lake Road, parents of other students would stop, open up their car doors, and take them to school. For Dylan it was just part of the magic of her childhood and something she forgot to tell her mom.

Everything shifted for her during her five years with us. She loved baking bread in an outdoor oven using flowerpots, collecting honey from the beehives, writing poetry, Kids Teaching Kids class, being in the plays, Women's Class, kick ball, wood carving, and hiking the trails during Wild Foods and Swamping. She loved the freedom and remembers the bouncy boards that were on huge spools and connected to an old sailboat. Inside that sailboat secrets were told and plots were hatched. She fell in love with the natural world. It just happened. She was no longer a city dweller; she was now a country girl.

One of the questions a prospective parent most often has is, What happens when a child leaves this small protected school and is enrolled in a public school? I attempt to answer this question and its thousand-and-one variations by noticing where the question is coming from. Depending on the context, I could focus my answer on how well our children do academically, or I can speak frankly about the social challenges kids have during this transition. I certainly can cite many success stories, including children who took it upon themselves to organize sports events, as well as former students who attended Harvard at one end of the spectrum, Ringling Bros. and Barnum & Bailey Clown College on the other.

When I recently asked Dylan about her transition, she said frankly, "It was devastating." She went from a school of fifty to a public high school with two thousand students located in Columbus, Indiana. She also went from living with her mother to living with her father. She found herself confronted with massive change, and she struggled. Her father helped her find the cross-country running team, and that helped mightily. She now had a small group of people that she could bond with who, like her, loved to run long distances. Although her love of running continues to nourish her to this day, during her high school days she suffered a severe weight loss, falling to just eighty-five pounds. Her cross-country coach insisted she gain weight in order to keep running, and that, coupled with guidance and support from friends and family, led her out of the darkness of an eating disorder.

She continued to struggle until just after her first year at Earlham College. Eventually, after a brief hospital stay and finding her major in biology, she came out the other side. She continues to run and to be out under the sky as often as possible. She has learned a few keys for sustaining her own happiness. One was that she loved field biology and would thrive working outside and not in a lab. The second thing she learned was that she was happiest when on skis, on the trail, on a bike, or in the water. She also learned that her life was in her hands, in her choices, in her heart, and living in community. When she runs, she smiles.

She met her husband Mitch in Colorado. They fell in love, and their love gave them a beautiful balance of adventure and music. Mitch went on a vision quest after reading *Be Here Now,* which is why he named his band Now is Now. He was impressed that Dylan knew all of the words to "Rocky Raccoon," one of his favorites, and a song she learned when she was seven. He might also be impressed that Ram Dass, who wrote *Be Here Now*, fell in love with Dylan's school and spent an entire weekend with our community just before his stroke.

They moved back east to be near the mountains. Dylan is the Back Country and Wilderness Supervisor of the White Mountain National Forest. She hikes ten to fourteen miles a day, sometimes alone, sometimes as a guide. Her job is to protect the wilderness, to make sure development does not creep into this forest, located just a day's drive from a huge knot of humanity. She loves her work, and she loves her life.

For the past eight years she has volunteered to coach a high school cross-country team. As they train to compete, Dylan encourages them to smile. They don't get this kind of advice from their other coach, but they do get the reason she encourages it. They train hard, and smiling takes them closer to joy.

Dylan has run three Boston marathons and finished two half triathlons. While training for one of the marathons, she woke one early spring morning to a mild snowstorm. She thought about letting go of the workout but decided to go for it. She started running and realized that she had left her stopwatch but continued running. She soon noticed that she had the road to herself. She opened her mouth to catch the soft, full snowflakes that were falling with an otherworldly gentleness. Her smile was huge and lit from within. She ran that morning as if she were one with the world. No race. No time. No people. No cars. No worry. No thing. She was having a direct experience with now is now.

Her cross-country team won last year. The state of Maine's principal association presents an award to the high school that has represented the highest form of sportsmanship. The state gave that award to Dylan's school. She loved this and so did they. She likes to point out that the biggest thing is not winning the race; it's getting along with one another. Perhaps her coaching is a way of connecting to her own high school experience and healing it. By serving others she brings her kindness, her sensitivity, her rich life experience to these kids who are vulnerable in the way she was when she left Upland Hills. She has found a way to intertwine five lines of intelligence that have formed the foundation of her hard-won happiness. Her love of the natural world, her love of her body in motion, her love of others, and her insights have all been set to music, thanks to Mitch.

When she was visiting her mom in Oregon, she noticed a wood cut that she had made for the school's calendar. The year was 1976. Her mom had framed her daughter's artwork and hung it on the wall. Dylan looked at it and noticed that it was a bird with four legs. She smiled and reflected. She had gone to a school where you could make a bird with hind legs and they found it worthy of publication. She smiled at the thought of her mythical bird who came from the forest of her childhood to remind her of the magic of those five years when she was an integral part of a wild school.

A Unique Line-Up of Intelligence Lines: Nina Raises Her Parents

When a child is born, we experience an intimate connection. As parents we hope and pray that our child will be born healthy and whole. We wait on pins and needles for that first breath and for the signs of wholeness, ten tiny fingers and ten small toes. We often experience a deep intimacy with the utter help-lessness of our newborn. We look at this fragile being, and the sheer weight of everything that led to this moment begins to sink in. Is it the huge responsibility of providing for, protect-ing, nourishing, and defending our child that causes our minds to race and our hearts to open? Or is it the memory of our distant ancestors that reaches out from the very beginnings of our species and taps us on the shoulder reminding us we were once stardust? Could it be that when a child is born the Great Mystery of life becomes personal and transcendent at the same time?

When I met Karen and John's daughter Nina, she was three-and-a-half years old. I had just turned twenty, still very close to my own childhood. I was attending Wayne State University at the time and deeply confused about who I was and where I was headed. I was drawn to Nina and wanted to know her from the moment we met. In some ways my parenting began that day, but it would be more accurate to say that her effect on me as a young, untested male, still in the throes of adolescence, was far more profound than anything I could ever offer her.

My intuition told me to watch her and to listen deeply. It told me to be patient and expressive. I was having direct experiences with a young being, and these experiences taught me to honor her worldview and to delight in the profound differences between her reality and mine. She helped me develop my empathy, kindness, humor, and tenderness, and in her presence I became alert.

By the time I married her mother about a year and a half later, I knew that I wanted to learn more about how children learn, and I knew that it was because of Nina. I graduated with a degree in education from Wayne State University, but my direct, daily interactions with Nina taught me more than I could have ever learned from an institution. Just as with our student David, it was poetry that eventually gave me an insight into the richness of Nina's inner world and into the stages of development that every child must inhabit, include, and transcend.

Forty years growing old
But still plopping
Plopping into chairs
On sunny afternoons
Newspaper
TV guide
Eating plump
Bible words
—Nina, age nine

By the time Nina was ready to leave our school at the age of thirteen, she had had her mother as a teacher for a year, and I was her teacher her last two years. Her learning profile looked something like this: She excelled in the area of interpersonal intelligence, evidenced by the quality and variety of her friend-ships and her relationships with adults. She showed uncommon depth in intrapersonal intelligence, evidenced by her poetry, journal writing, and self-evaluations. She was highly motivated in language arts, loved to read, and was an exceptional writer.

However, Nina had difficulty with math as soon as she moved beyond simple arithmetic. She struggled with the idea that she needed to learn algebra and geometry. She also had difficulty with word problems that included many variables. When she turned twenty-seven and was waitressing at a bar in Ann Arbor, something clicked. She was holding cash and need-ing to be her own "bank" as the night unfolded, and suddenly it all made sense to her. Her line of mathematics and logic lit up. By the time she studied for her real-estate license she was now doing more complex problem-solving, always within the con-text of earning money. She was interested in music, loved the natural world, had a natural instinct for picture smarts, and en-joyed throwing a Frisbee, but they were secondary to her true passions. Her passion was in language, people, cultivating her rich interior space, and creativity. She liked exploring big ideas and probing into the big questions of life, which is the line of the existentialist, but it was clear to us, her parents, where her passions were.

Nina's development helped me to appreciate how every child has a unique learning profile. The most important thing for us as parents was her excitement and passion about learn-ing. She loved going to school, and she worked hard at doing well. She was very kind and sensitive to others, and she could interact with a wide variety of children and adults.

Our job as her parents was to do our best to protect her gifts and to encourage her to be true to who she was without any attachment to specific outcomes or agendas. The essence of conscious parenting is to learn how to let go and to use the rich experience of parenting to work on ourselves to become better human beings.

She was an avid reader, and we noticed how much she loved books about families. The Melendy Family series by Elizabeth Enright were a favorite of hers and so were the Little House on the Prairie books by Laura Ingalls Wilder. She loved Friday night dinners at her nana Jean's house, where the large dining-room table would be filled with an ever-shifting group of family and friends. Friday night dinners were a weekly event that were filled with a random assortment of main dishes all lovingly prepared by my mother, and Nina looked forward to them.

But it is only in retrospect we can say that her central calling was to become a mother of five children. Her devotion to raising her children and to providing the richest atmosphere possible for each of them to become who they were meant to be was not something that we could have predicted as she was developing. The adult Nina has three degrees from major universities and her real-estate license; she is a talented and skilled writer; and beyond all of those her life's energy is centered on the fullness of her family.

This fullness is what pioneering psychologist Carol Gilligan, a former student of Lawrence Kohlberg, identified when she developed her theory of care-based morality. Care-based morality emphasizes universality and inter-connectedness. It is thought to be more common in girls because of their connections to their mothers. The post-conventional stage emphasizes universal care for self and for others.

Now as a mother, Nina is finding an abundance of meaning and growth in all lines of intelligence as her five children each have their own unique profile. Their individual "diversity" has sparked Nina to grow in areas that were not as interesting to her when she was a child and unmarried adult. Her current fulfillment is directly related to her role as a mother of five who has also adopted a sixth child, who is a young adult. She finds in conscious parenting a total direct experience with learning about and living lessons that are connected to love, interrelatedness, and nonviolence.

Developmental Beings and Becomings

When we take the perspective that all children are developmental beings, we enter into an appreciation of how complex and interesting children truly are. As a child grows and matures, she can express different kinds of beings at different stages. It's almost as if your child wakes up one year and sees and experiences her world from a changed beingness—and if your connection with your child is strong, you do too. That is how being a parent allows us to deepen and broaden our own lines of intelligence. It challenges us to grow into greater consciousness, and it, more than anything else, prepares us for the great unknown of tomorrow.

The grandfathers and grandmothers of developmental theory have paved the way for us to re-think, re-design, and re-imagine schools, parenting, culture, and the future. They have given us a road map to become more compassionate, more caring, more skilled, and more fulfilled.

We now have a greater appreciation for children as our teachers, as potential, and as developmental beings. We have seen some compelling examples of how identifying, cultivating, and nurturing a child's unique genius can unfold into a fulfilling adulthood that involves both individual expression and service to others. There is yet another way a child's life can be woven into a larger context, and that is through rites of passage. As you will see in the next chapter, we intentionally created certain rites of passage as part of our school culture, and sometimes unanticipated life events became rites of passage, because we contextualized them that way.

Children of the future who are empowered by rites of passage will integrate life lessons and acquire the tools for living in these complex and uncertain times. These children will grow into adults who experience life as a deeply connected experience of infinite creativity infused with complicated challenges that have life-and-death consequences. As Bucky used to say, "Utopia or Oblivion."

Chapter Five

RITES OF PASSAGE

So remember take up courage and have patience, and endurance, and alertness; these four things you have to have to be an Earth Person.

—*Wallace Black Elk*

The paradox of raising a child is realizing that in the end it is all about learning to let them go. We protect, foster, nurture, nourish, and defend our children in order to help them individuate and develop the strength and confidence to become full participants in the adult world. Our hope is that our child will have the heart, the tools, and the courage to live a life of meaning and purpose. We may have specific ideas about their success and happiness, but if we align on the idea that we want our children to become who they were meant to be, then our ideas will shift and change as our children grow into their young adult years and beyond.

From a child's first step we understand that once they can motor under their own steam, they're off. Children are natural explorers; they're designed that way. Bucky Fuller used to talk about testing what he called "portal number one," the mouth, which is where an exploring toddler puts things. (Interestingly, perhaps that's why the tonsils are the first checkpoint of the immune system. Western medicine, not understanding this, has made them expendable.) Bucky also marveled at the ingenious design of soft, cushy buttocks designed to break the fall of a toddler learning to stand or walk, our own built-in airbags.

All these "safety devices" are required because children are naturally driven by a profound curiosity about any and every thing around them. We currently live in times where there is so much fear about potential kidnapping, abuse, neglect, car accidents, and a whole list of silent and potentially dangerous health threats that we have forgotten our own childhoods, and the fact that our job is both to protect and to encourage.

Our Daughter Is Transmuted

One summer morning when our daughter Sasha was ten years old, she went missing. I was on duty at the time. I had noticed that she was either very quietly working in her room on a huge jigsaw puzzle, or she had left the house. It was not uncommon for her to spend cherished alone time in nature or in her room, but after three hours without seeing her or hearing from her I became concerned. I checked every spot inside our home and then went to the school to see if I could find her. I began to call her name and after searching around and inside of school decided to head towards the Ecological Awareness Center.

I paused at the top of the hill leading to the center and noticed a teepee on the crest of the next hill. As I approached the teepee, I heard a deep resonant voice. I entered quietly and looked around. That voice belonged to a Lakota man with two black braids and a face weathered by time, sun, and wind. He was speaking in English with many Lakota words, and seven other people were listening intently. Next to him sat a woman who was using a bead loom as she listened, and next to her was Sasha doing the same thing. I sat down and listened too and entered into a strange new world of story, spirit, space, and mystery.

Wallace Black Elk was a descendant of a visionary, Nicholas Black Elk, the author of *Black Elk Speaks*. He used language in a way I had never heard before. I'd be following along understanding this bit and that, and then I'd hear something that would challenge my logical mind so badly that I'd give up. We were mesmerized by his voice, his wisdom, his laughter, and his mind.

I had no idea how he found us or even why he was here; I just had to let go and be present. For Sasha it was the only place she wanted to be. She would get up each morning and head to the teepee. Lisa, who taught her how to bead, took care of her, and Sasha blossomed in her presence. They stayed for an entire week, and people came from all over to hear Wallace teach and to enter into the sweat lodge together to purify and pray.

He gave us direct experiences that helped us to heal, to let go, and to enter into sacred time. We always sat in a circle. We learned how to pray out loud. We learned how to pray with another's voice. We learned how to invite the four directions into our consciousness. We learned how to smoke the chanupa. We learned some Lakota words, and we learned how to sing the prayer songs. We were invited to take actions on behalf of Mother Earth and to help others learn how to respect, honor, heal, and care for her. We were cautioned about how to use the sweat lodge and to always have a pipe holder or a sun dancer pour. Wallace shared his visions, and he told us about vision quest, and he promised us that someday a man would come who would teach us how to quest, how to build drums, and how to become a sun dancer.

The day before they left Lisa asked me a question that shook and challenged my western mind. She told me that she had adopted Sasha and explained to me that it simply meant that Sasha would always be in her heart. I smiled. Then she asked if she could take Sasha with her for an entire year and give me her son in exchange. Inside my mind every word, every thought, every feeling said, "Are you crazy?" But I paused long enough to feel the beauty of her request. I declined her generous invitation but never forgot it.

During this school year of 1983–1984, our school enrollment shrunk to its lowest level. The economy in Detroit was suffering through a recession; parents wanted us to redesign our program so that children could participate in just the afternoons. Our staff pulled together to take on more responsibility for less pay. Doubts about the viability of our school arose every day, and I often thought about throwing in the towel. But at the very same time people showed up like Wallace, and time after time we were reminded to value the essence of what we were trying to co-create. At its core we were re-inventing not just school but how to live lives of meaning rooted in community. We were experiencing our rite of passage through a difficult decade, and it tested our resolve and our resilience. Wallace Black Elk's words, "Remember, take up courage and have patience, and endurance and alertness; these four things you have to have to be an Earth Person" helped us to navigate the dangerous waters of a difficult time.

Designing Rites of Passage

There are field trips, and then there are rites of passage. A field trip is an excursion to somewhere, usually with an educational component. A rite of passage offers an opportunity to develop and stretch yourself from the inside out. It is a subjective dive into your inner realms.

Rites of passage for children can begin at a very early age and provide creative and powerful ways for children to gain confidence and to learn about risk taking. At our school we have rites-of-passage trips built in for each of the six morning meetings that span the ages of four to fourteen. As we designed these trips, we realized the importance of each one and how to cater to the specific needs of that stage of development so that the experience challenged and stretched the children yet was well within their power. For instance, our youngest group is composed of twelve children who range in age from a mature four year old to a sturdy five year old. This is the only group in our school where the parents have the option of sending their child for half days. The stages of each rite of passage include at least these three distinct elements: preparation, the journey, and the return.

For the first group, the teacher prepares by selecting a journey and organizing the parts of the journey that will challenge them while fully supporting their success. The children and their parents are told about the journey and how important and special it is. The preparation for this journey is focused on a sunhat that each child decorates and keeps. The hat becomes the child's memory object that serves the purpose of providing shade on the longest group hike of the year. Because the school is located on Upland Hills Farm, a demonstration farm that has lots of farm animals, several playgrounds, three barns, a pond, and a picnic area, the youngest children never have to leave the property to experience their adventure.

On the last day of school the children gather with their backpacks, sunhats, and water bottles to hike from our school to the farm, a little less than a mile. They set off on this journey as if they were crossing a great chasm. By the time they reach the school apple-tree parking lot, one of the kids is already tired and squeaky. The others help by offering water, and the teacher keeps them all moving. They reach a halfway point at the highest part of Upland Hills Farm, a place we call Bonfire Hill. They pause there for water and cherries, and while sitting on a log they spontaneously begin a game of seeing who can spit the cherry pit the furthest. The trek continues past the community-supported agriculture area, and we recognize a friend who is planting and weeding. She comes over to smile and encourage the children as they now can finally see their destination. When the children arrive, at least one of their family members is there to join them, and even though they just saw them a few hours ago they delight in meeting them after their long walk. Once at the farm they participate in a farm show, where they learn about shearing a sheep and milking a cow. The trip culminates in a story about the invisible thread that connects their hearts one to another. They listen carefully as their teacher talks about how this thread will connect them long after this day ends, and as she finishes the story she makes a simple thread bracelet for each child.

They board a hay wagon, and as they pass the pathway to our school their teacher gets off and waves goodbye. The children continue with their parents, and summer begins.

This simple rite-of-passage example has all the elements in it that will follow this child until they graduate at the age of thirteen or fourteen. The preparation, the journey, and the return are there as a repeating pattern that will serve to remind each child about their ability to cross over into new territory. This also serves as a reminder to us as parents and as teachers that children are under our care for a very short time and that our job is to raise them to the best of our abilities and to let them go so that they can find their way in the world and improve it in some way.

By the time the child reaches our third group, as mature seven-year-olds to young nine-year-olds, the rite of passage is designed around an overnight. This rite of passage invites the child to sleep away from home, to get to their destination on their own power, to trust in each other, and to discover the silence, beauty, and wonder of the natural world. Their teacher introduces the date of the trip only two weeks before it happens. We have learned from experience that the children and parents experience less anxiety when the trip is almost upon them. The teacher sends home the permission slip, and each child begins the journey of making the choice. The children's curiosity builds each day as one after another decides to attend. This last year Alex declared as the permission slip was being handed out, "I'm not going." Class members offered some encouragement, but Alex was certain that sleeping with a bunch of people in a cabin, on a bunk bed, was not for him. The journey has already begun before one step is taken on the trail. During the weeks proceeding, bunk-bed models will be built out of wood blocks; the children will choose their bunk, change their minds, plan the meals, make lists, move from a top bunk to the middle, buy flashlights, cheer when a permission slip comes in, and learn what the word outhouse means.

On a spring day in May the children set off from school on foot to walk the three miles through Upland Hills Farm and onto state land where one foot trail leads to another until they arrive at the Tamarack Cabins. As they begin their walk, their teacher has selected places for stopping to drink, where wonder and enchantment can unfold. There's the stop at the apple tree for a group picture, a stop at Ken's field to find the perfect long grass for hand whistling, and the stop where their teacher gets on all fours as the children one at a time jump over her. They stop at the bottom of a hill and turn like whirling dervishes and then try to run to the top, and just as they approach their destination they play "boats in the ocean" among a stand of tall pine trees. They arrive at the cabins proud of their accomplishment and ready to eat the food that they helped to prepare.

This particular rite of passage was developed over time by one of our founding teachers, whom I had first met as an asthmatic camper when he was just ten years old. His childhood vulnerabilities and the way he triumphed over them are apparent in his design. The elements of getting there on your own, traveling a distance, jumping over hurdles, making the journey more important than the destination, the power of being in the now to trump anxiety, and sleeping in a new place all relate to the challenges he faced as a child. His gift as a teacher was to create an overnight trip that helped children to overcome their fears and perceived limitations. But perhaps the most compelling intention of this trip is to have the group discover and experience the joy of belonging to a group.

This last year the group consisted of sixteen children. The temperament of the group was influenced deeply by the fact that at least six of these children are healers. During my tenure I have often noticed that certain children have the ability to help other children heal psychological wounds. These children are deeply sensitive and empathetic. They notice a child who is eating alone, and they go over to join them. They sense when a child is struggling to communicate, and they offer patience. They are attracted to resolving conflict when it arises and are determined to return to the kind of play that includes everyone. This group was unique in that there was a center of gravity formed by the core of these compassionate kids.

The group also included two outliers: Alex and Maggie. Alex is someone who does not like change and is often noncompliant. He enjoys being alone and is afraid of failing. He is often oppositional and requires extraordinary patience. Maggie has Down syndrome and is older than the other children. She has some difficulty being understood and often makes self-soothing sounds when involved in an activity and has never slept away from home. Maggie is joyful and thrives on adult attention and is deeply connected to her teacher. Alex's parents wanted him to go on the trip, which was one of the reasons he didn't want to go. His classmates encouraged him day after day and without pressure, having learned that Alex needs space to make a decision. His father offered to come on the trip, and Alex agreed. Maggie's mother signed on to come on the trip as well, and this set the stage for the unexpected result.

It's early evening, and a campfire has started; the children are gathered around the fire, and Maggie stands up and says, "Everyone, everyone, listen to me." Her words are clear and her intention clearer, and as the children begin to listen, she puts her finger in front of her mouth and starts to shush, shush. Her eyes are bright, and perhaps she is feeling strong because even though many people had their doubts that she'd be able to walk the three miles, she did it and knew it.

The kids get quiet, and her teacher offers a silent prayer on Maggie's behalf.

"I want to sing a song, and I want you to sing with me," she says.

Her teacher thinks, "Maggie please have a song in mind, and make it one that they know."

Maggie starts, "Doe, a deer, a female deer . . ." and the children all join in, and they sing the song with Maggie as the leader, and she glows.

Alex's dad watches as his son often chooses to be on his own and to be looking for something small on the forest floor. He notices how patient and loving Alex's teacher is, and he also notices how understanding Alex's classmates are and how often they invite him to join them.

By the time they walk back to school with no stops, tired, happy, and triumphant, they have crossed an invisible chasm.

They are the same children who posed for the picture by the apple tree, but something powerful has changed in each one of them. They have become a group. They belong to each other and to a place. They have the power to heal and to include. They have experienced something that no test can measure. They know they are capable of moving beyond the familiar boundaries of their home and their school. They belong to a future that is based in love.

The oldest two morning-meeting groups build on the foundations that the younger groups have encouraged and demonstrated. For over two decades our fifth morning-meeting group, sixteen children who are eleven and twelve years old, have taken a weeklong trip to an island. Their teacher had taught two comprehensive units that centered on water. The first comprehensive unit was called "Voyage of the Mimi," a thirteen-episode American educational television program depicting the crew of the Mimi exploring the ocean and taking a census of humpback whales. The second comprehensive unit she taught had to do with early American history as seen through the eyes of Native Americans and settlers. Life in the mid-1800s was a central focus of their study, and they learned how essential water was in determining the success of a tribe or a town. In order to integrate these two thematic units and bring them to life, she found an extraordinary university professor from Central Michigan University, who was delighted with the idea of opening up his research station in early May, on Beaver Island, by hosting our group of fifth and sixth graders.

For many years this charismatic teacher delighted our children with hikes and adventures that included finding all seven species of snakes on the island, catching fish by using your hands, discovering the mysteries of a bog, and the trip highlight: his hour-long program on the tuatara, a reptile found only in New Zealand. Now the children were not only sleeping away from their homes, they were living on an island far away from their familiar world, surrounded by the buildings and burial mounds of the very time they had studied. They discovered how to live and learn together in a communal way, and they delighted in their bond as they discovered the joys of island life. They flourished in an environment dedicated to university students, and they experienced the joy and independence that comes from being treated like a college student rather than a fifth grader.

The cumulative experience of more than twenty years of this rite-of-passage trip has led many of our former students to pursue ways of integrating their lives with their passions. Listening to Jim as he wove his spell, watching him as he pulled snakes out of the strangest places, feeling his delight and wonder as he tramped off into a swamp, our students experienced passion at its best. Passion and place, living on an island, life as an adventure, communal living, and a week of time out of time all combine to offer insights into each other and ourselves.

When Jim retired, his program suffered so much that we needed to reinvent the rite of passage for this group. We knew that the essential elements from our Beaver Island trip would form the foundation for this new trip, but now we needed to use our imaginations and contacts to find a new place and a new person for our children to experience. This age group, mature ten-year-olds to young twelve-year-olds, is ready for a big adventure, yet they need a clear structure and a guiding purpose. It took their teacher two to three years before she discovered an experience that included all of the essential elements of the Beaver Island trip and transcended to a new level.

The Camp Arbutus trip is a five-day trip that includes sailing, science, South Manitou Island, a shipwreck, and a huge sand dune. The sum total of the experience leads directly to self-confidence and self-esteem.

Our oldest group, Ted's group, sets the tone for the entire school. We teach leadership at our school, and this group is given the responsibility of becoming leaders for the entire school. One working definition for the kind of leadership we teach is someone who motivates people to fulfill their highest potential by offering them opportunities, rather than obligations.

Once a student reaches Ted's group, the entire two years can be seen as a series of rites of passages. The first bonding trip is the Stratford Trip. This two-day, one-night journey takes advantage of how close our school is to Canada. The trip leaves our school at noon and returns the following day by early evening. It requires a passport and the reading of one of Shakespeare's plays. The experience includes crossing a bridge, entering a new country, arriving in a city that sustains itself by celebrating and presenting live theatrical productions, viewing two plays, eating out, and returning. It gives our students an opportunity to experience artists at the height of their craft within the context of learning about great literature. Because our school celebrates and infuses the curriculum with the creative and performing arts, this town and this trip has become a peak experience for many of our kids.

The second trip for Ted's group is the Chicago Trip. Here again our students are presented with the opportunity to travel to a city that is culturally rich. The preparation for this trip involves learning about the history of Chicago, deciding which live theatrical event they will attend, and learning about train travel. The idea behind this trip is to emphasize travel without using a car. They gather to depart from the Royal Oak train station and from there ride into the Windy City, where they walk to their hotel and learn to use public transportation until they return to the station they departed from. This experience is designed to empower the students to navigate a travel experience that contrasts with the way that most of them have been used to all of their lives.

The final senior trip for the oldest morning-meeting group challenges the students to raise their own money for a class treasury that will be used for senior projects and the senior trip. Their teacher is dedicated to teaching his students the value of money, the value of work and consistency, the power of doing something that you are passionate about, and the discipline that is required to succeed. For over twenty years he has modeled these values and designed his curriculum around how to make the transition from our school to the next one.

Ted is a professional musician, a licensed builder, and most importantly an openhearted and open-minded teacher. He wanted to create something that would be the equivalent to an individual rite of passage to complement the series of group rites of passages. He defined a senior project as a student-driven process from start to finish that would support the learner in creating something that they were passionate about. The process would begin during the fall when his graduating students would develop an idea, talk about it with their classmates, and eventually pitch it to the entire staff. At the staff meeting the student's idea would be discussed, and a mentor from the staff would be assigned to assist the student from that point forward.

The range of ideas that the students have executed over the years include building a small sailboat to recording a CD of music written and composed by the student. Each idea has contributed to our whole school culture of taking an initiative, learning from your mistakes, overcoming obstacles, and completing the project.

The final rite of passage for our oldest students includes all of the aspects of the other rites-of-passage trips and transcends to a new level of group and individual empowerment.

The trip is called Camp Lookout. The students have raised all of the funds for this trip, so there's no cost. The three-night, four-day trip begins by dividing up all of the meals between different students who organize the menu for the entire group. There are vegan diets, gluten-free diets, allergies, and whole-food preferences to account for. The trip itself has evolved into an experience of work and play. Camp Lookout is located in the beautiful Leelanau Peninsula of Michigan, a four-hour drive from our school. Our school opens the camp for the season and is responsible for all of the work required in lieu of payment. So every morning is devoted to completing the group tasks assigned for that day. The morning is about earning your keep, and the afternoon and evenings are free for enjoyment. Because Camp Lookout is accessible only by boat, the group must be fully prepared for the four-day adventure. Once there, the trip becomes a metaphor for living the good life.

Which translates into, once the work is completed, play becomes the entire focus. The group learns the value of one another and how the natural world can become an endless path to enjoyment. This extended time away from all technology and their familiar surroundings leads to an unwinding and an emptying out of the collected stresses of everyday routines. The group bonds deeply just before the school year is over, and an appreciation of each other becomes apparent as their time runs out.

On a trip like this the simple things become so important: laughter, music, fires on the beach, storytelling, dancing, running, playing, bike riding, climbing sand dunes, cooking together, and swimming in Lake Michigan become the conduit for celebrating the learning community that they have formed through the year and throughout in some cases nine or ten years of Upland Hills School.

A Child's Death

In April of 1977, my patience and my soul were tested. This test demanded that I use everything I had learned up until that point from my own childhood and from my own children, as well as from the children I had adopted into my heart during the first six years of our young school. It challenged us all, and it tested our ideas and our ideals. I can remember it clearly; it literally and metaphorically drove me to my knees. I was twenty-eight years old.

It was one of the first true spring days of 1977. The sun was out, and the temperature broke seventy, reminding us that winter's grip might finally be over. I was repairing one of the doors on our portable classroom, marveling at how warped this metal door had become. Then I thought about how many times I had seen one of the older boys attempt a kung fu kick to the breakaway hardware and realized it was a minor miracle that the door had not flown off its flimsy hinges. Then from the direction of the parking lot I heard someone yelling my name over and over again. I placed the vise grip down and walked in the direction of the alarmed voice.

"Come quick, there's been an accident!"

I drove the less than two miles to a devastating scene. I could see children scattered along the roadside and hear their shouts of pain and crying amid stunned silence. I saw our Dodge Maxi-Van on its side and tried to find the child who seemed to be in the most pain. I went over to Brian and put him in my lap, and as I held him he began to calm down. As he settled into my arms, I looked around me to assess the situation. Melissa had her sister Kim by her side and was bleeding from her head; Michael was mangled and in great pain but had Laurel, who he called "Toad," by his side; and Jonathon was screaming while his sister Beth did what she could to comfort her six-and-a-half-year-old brother. I then noticed a green army coat over a body.

We waited there until the ambulance came, and I watched as the crew decided who needed to get to the hospital first. I told them about Michael, who was suffering silently, and we carried Brian into the ambulance and rode directly to the emergency room. During the ride I noticed that Melissa had an open head injury; Michael was lucky just to be alive; Brian and Jonathon had broken bones, but it was hard to know if that was the extent of their injuries. The phone in the ambulance kept falling off of its cradle because of the condition of Lake George Road and the urgent speed of our vehicle. When the ambulance doors opened, the hospital staff was waiting, and they took Melissa and Michael directly to the operating room. Brian and Jonathon were also taken for treatment, and I waited by the emergency-room door to determine the condition of the rest of the riders. Within an hour we knew that Melissa and Michael were in the greatest danger and everyone else was intact, everyone else except for one who was dead.

The first parent who came through the door was a good friend and the father of Beth and Jonathon. I greeted him with an embrace and told him that they were fine and that Jonathon had a collarbone injury and Beth minor bruises. He pulled back from the embrace and asked how I was. I told him I didn't know, and then as if he were reading my thoughts he said, "The school has to continue."

I collapsed.

During so many moments of the unfolding trauma, I had been playing an internal tape that repeated, "It's over, this is the worst thing that could happen, it's over. We'll never come back from this, this is the end of the school."

Jim's words, "The school has to continue," broke me open and let me release the emotions that I had been feeling ever since I heard the first child's scream of pain. Jim picked me up, and a nurse came over to me and asked if I was the director of the school. I said yes, and she asked if I could be present with the parents of the child who had been killed. I was stunned by this request and asked her their names, and when she said "The Kaplan's," I knew then for the first time that it was Scott under that green army jacket.

I walked over to Mort and Esther and embraced them both as we walked to a small room with a closed door. The nurse opened the door, and there was Scott, lifeless on a table without his glasses. There were no words spoken. I looked at his eleven-year-old lifeless body and couldn't believe that his life force had left. He was one of the most animated alive children I had ever known. Whenever we were down on the farm and the draft horses were needing to be driven from the barn to the pasture, Scott would join two adults jumping up and down yelling, "Ha, ha!" at the top of his lungs with his little arms up in the air. The horses responded and did exactly as he asked, and in that moment he wasn't the special-ed kid who struggled with reading; he was cowboy Scott who could wrangle draft horses from barn to pasture.

We stayed in silence for a time, and then I walked them to their car in shock, and as they drove away, I fell one more time to the ground.

Scott has remained my teacher ever since. He taught me patience, the "long patience" that involved experiencing the grief and loss in the wake of his death. He taught me about forgiveness. He taught me to cherish each moment as he did with vitality and delight. He taught me about impermanence and the things we cannot change. He became my life companion. His form and his life left that day but not his essence. I discovered that the memories that I have of his childhood have been elevated in my mind to a position of core importance. His unlikely friendship with David showed me how children can become healers. He introduced me to the true power of community. His death and the accident brought our community together in unbelievable ways. The many acts of kindness, from food baskets on our doorstep to the healing laughter that Michael's mother and I shared the day we learned he would be all right, join a flood of memories that knitted us together in a new and resilient way.

Melissa was operated on by an esteemed brain surgeon who had to meticulously take out every grain of sand and stone in her brain. When he closed the area, we had to wait to see if Melissa would come back to herself or face a life forever impaired in some way. Over the course of her slow recovery, a steady stream of family and community members visited Melissa. She slowly regained her speech and memory and was making progress. Her doctor paid special attention to her. He met many of the parents from our school in the process and was so struck with their love and concern he eventually enrolled his son. Melissa came back before school was out that year. Her brave smile and her courage, her shaved head and her ability to connect helped each of us in our own healing. She is currently a nurse.

Michael was operated on many times. The doctors were cautiously confident of his recovery, but he had sustained many internal injuries. His kidney and liver were damaged, as were just about every other internal organ. He had been thrown to the back doors of the vehicle and was pinched, half in and half out, as the van rolled two and a half times. It took almost six months for him to gain a release from the hospital, and then, just as he was about to be released, they discovered his eyeball's nerve had been pinched. A doctor had to hold his eyeball with a forceps and pull it in hopes of releasing the nerve. During this same time, his brother Chris almost died of fever and needed to be packed in ice. Michael's parents decided to move to Hawaii, and by the beginning of 1978 they were on the island of Maui healing and beginning new lives. Michael made a complete recovery. He is currently a builder, an architect, inventor, musician, and visionary who credits the school with inspiring him to live sustainably. He has been involved with installing massive solar projects and electrical-vehicle charging stations throughout the island of Maui.

The children of the bus accident were teachers for our entire community. That particular group of souls went out into the world and changed it. They would become emblematic of the kinds of children our school would work with going forward. First and foremost they were diverse. Michael, Scott, and David all had experienced some form of special education before attending Upland Hills School. Each of them enriched our lives beyond measure. Michael's sense of humor, his inventiveness, his passion for making things, and his determination flourished during his time at our school. He found his voice and his future after feeling hopeless and deeply inadequate due to his previous schooling experiences. Scott woke up at our school. He formed a friendship with David that broke down David's wall to the world and gave David the permission to laugh, to write poetry, to be led into adventures, and to know the warmth and kindness of true friendship. David in turn taught us to be open and to let go of preconceived ideas of what a Down syndrome child could or couldn't do. His smile was worth a million dollars. He didn't use it often, but when he did it changed the light.

Beth and Jonathon are both parents and lawyers, having graduated from the University of Michigan and Harvard respectively. Beth has a very important job using her law degree to help insure equal opportunity for minorities. But for me, hearing her explain why she wanted her children to attend a charter school in Brooklyn that is known for mainstreaming special-education children warmed my heart and reminded me of her ease with her fellow classmates, and her love and appreciation for them.

The children involved in the accident taught me how to walk through darkness. Had I had followed my own promptings, I would've given up, but because of them I didn't. The accident happened on a Friday, and on the Monday following we gathered together as a whole school. We began our all-school meeting with a song, "The Michigan Tall Trees"—"I want to wake up in the morning where the Michigan tall trees grow." We came together to sing and to share our grief and our sadness. We gathered to remember Scott and to hold on to each other. We gathered outside and were joined by the beauty of a Michigan spring. Jim was right. The school must continue, and it did.

Scott's life and death taught an entire community to appreciate a child who is happy. It certainly wasn't Scott's grades, his age, or his accomplishments that lived on; it was his essence, his delight, his persistence, his sense of humor, his imagination, his curiosity, and his smile. He taught us that love is stronger than death.

My experience of that April day lives as the day I went from young adulthood into maturity. I played a mental loop while in shock, in that emergency waiting room, a loop that said, "It's over, it's over, run away, run away." Jim's hug and his words that have lived beyond his lifetime dispelled that mental trap. It was not my choice to decide whether the school would continue; it was beyond my choice, my knowing, and my experience. Death teaches us about impermanence, and it never leaves. I passed through this time by learning how to receive kindness, by listening to others, by mourning Scott's loss, and by facing the next day.

It's Your World Now:
Glenn Frey

Travel experiences can also be possible rites of passage because they're like putting on a new set of lenses or gateways to new worlds and new perspectives. A century ago, it was not uncommon for people to be born, to marry, to have children, and to die without leaving their small town or village. Today, we can be continually "reincarnated" in the same body as we experience new and life-changing experiences. In the spring of 2008, thanks to a series of synchronous events, our school was given the opportunity to travel to Mexico City. The origins of this trip reach back to the winter of 1961 when I entered junior high school.

It was at Clara Barton Junior High School in Royal Oak Michigan that I met a boy who would not only change my life but also eventually change the world. We were sitting in a gymnasium waiting for our turn to wrestle. The physical education department of all of the junior high schools in our district was sponsoring a school-wide wrestling contest to determine winners in every weight class. Having three brothers, one older and two younger, I was well acquainted with grabbing or being grabbed, throwing or being thrown, and pinning or being pinned. However, as a Jewish kid living near the National Shrine of the Little Flower, home to the notoriously anti-Semitic radio priest Father Coughlin, I had already learned to be wary of non-Jews who wanted to fight. I would be wrestling at the 103-pound weight class, and the guy sitting to my left would be wrestling at the "featherweight" class, which meant he weighed even less than me and we would not be wrestling each other.

We started talking to each other out of curiosity and nervousness. He seemed to know that I might be a Jewish kid, and

I was attracted to his sense of humor. He asked me if it were true that all Jewish girls behaved as if they were princesses, and I laughed when he turned his head slightly upward with an air of disdain. He was easy to talk to and very curious. He was then summoned to the mat before me; he went out there and within minutes had his opponent on his back; three slaps on the mat by the ref and he was back victorious. My opponent looked like his arms had two more muscles than mine; I lasted until the end of the match but lost on points.

My new friend was enrolled in a special class that was known as the Major Workroom, a class for creative kids who showed promise in the arts. I had a friend in that class and was impressed by the freedom and creativity that the kids had in contrast to the drab routine of my daily schedule. As adults we talked about his experience in the Major Workroom and how it was the highlight of his educational life and in fact was the only time he really felt alive in school.

When I went off to Michigan State University, he went to Los Angeles to found one of the most successful rock groups of all time. We have kept in touch over the years, and after a visit to LA he called me to offer his services in order to raise money for our school. This is how Glenn Frey, the founder of the band the Eagles, led us to the Starkey Hearing Foundation, which through its founder, Bill Austin, has created missions throughout the world to bring the gift of hearing to those in need.

Upland Hills School received a generous donation from the Starkey Hearing Foundation that was used to form the seed of a tuition-assistance program. Independent schools like ours are always in need of attracting and maintaining our enrollments so that we can maintain cultural and economic diversity while meeting our yearly budgets. The foundation also supported us in hosting a daylong mission in the heart of Detroit's cultural center to bring the gift of hearing to over six hundred Detroiters. Yet it was the invitation to bring ten members of our community on a mission to Mexico City that created a rite of passage that would change our lives and the lives of the people we met.

American scholar Joseph Campbell, who wrote *The Hero with a Thousand Faces*, was a remarkable teacher who synthesized the hero's journey after a lifelong study of myths from all over the world. His work became popularized through a remarkable television series produced by the Public Broadcasting Service called *The Power of Myth* that was first aired in 1988. When Joe taught workshops on this topic, he often chose Jean Houston to assist in dramatizing and deepening the content of each workshop or lecture. Jean is currently using the hero's journey in a new context. She believes, as I do, that the hero's journey is now a collective and collaborative affair. We need to discover not only our individual purpose in life, but this current time, that Jean calls "the time of the parenthesis," demands that we learn how to actualize as groups.

We took ten people to Mexico City with all expenses paid by the Starkey Hearing Foundation. This rite of passage offered us the opportunity to live aspects of our mission in a deeply profound way. In our mission statement we talk about "making friends with people around the world." What better way to live that aspect of our mission than by traveling to another country with the intention of bringing the gift of hearing to people who could not afford to buy hearing aids?

In preparation for our trip we needed to develop a criterion for prospective candidates who would offer the best of our community. The qualities that we looked for were compassion, service, social intelligence, hard work, and kindness. We selected the candidates through recommendations, interviews, and years of personal interactions. Our team of adults and students was also selected to emphasize collaboration, and we invited a diverse group that would be able to meet obstacles and overcome adversity.

Once we arrived in Mexico City, the adventure offered us a perfect blend of learning and giving. We walked to many of our destinations, and through the kindness and generosity of Bill and Tani Austin of the Starkey Hearing Foundation, we were treated to a rich variety of historical, cultural, and entertaining offerings. But at the center of our five-day experience was the mission to assist in delivering as many hearing aids to as many people as possible. This required us to be trained by the Starkey team and to work closely under the supervision of their audiologists. People came from hundreds of miles and waited patiently for hours as our team worked. It was a humbling and deeply moving experience. I worked with a former student who was known for his gentle manner and hard work. Together with the aid of a trained audiologist we fit over a hundred people during our sessions. There was a ninety-seven-year-old woman who embraced us and said that she would pray for us every day for the rest of her life. There was a child who laughed and cried when her silence ended.

That mission assisted 1,014 people. It also demonstrated to each of us how giving and receiving is the way that love takes a breath. It changed each of us in subtle and profound ways. One member of our team has pursued audiology as a career. The rest of us will never forget that the chasm of language, culture, class, and poverty can be crossed when love is present. This rite of passage connected us to one of the most interesting and dynamic cities on earth while giving us the chance to travel with purpose and meaning.

Glenn Frey's music used harmony and poetry to communicate beyond his lifetime. He lived with such intensity it was as if he knew he had to get it all in before it was too late. He sensed that a song could easily outlive a human being. When he was thirteen, his essence was already in place. He was curious, funny, engaging, and driven to please a father whom he never really knew. When we met in Los Angeles, he would let go of his finely crafted persona and open up his heart. He talked about his kids and how challenging it was to be a parent. He had come to parenting late in life and was discovering the complexities of parenting in the twenty-first century. He was now a father of three children and just as engaged and bewildered as the rest of us. During one of our LA visits, he gave me a CD that he made with his kids, and I thought about how he was using this line of intelligence to heal his wounds and to bond with his children. During his last tour, he called me and left a message, inviting to invite me to come backstage. His voice was tired and thin, perhaps a morning-after voice, perhaps the end of a long run. The thing about that last voice message that moved me the most was that he gave me access to his direct phone line. In his world it meant more than "I trust you;" it meant there was a possibility of closer relatedness. He left this advice to our granddaughter , who was equivocating about going whether to go to college or touring for a year. It was pure Glenn.

Please tell that beautiful and talented young lady Ii say go for it!
You can always go back to school.
Right now your dreams are more important and the education you'll get is worth a hundred diplomas.
I wish for you all the love and luck the gods will allow.
Work hard and be self- critical.
There are thousands of bad songwriters in the world. Most of 'em in Nashville.
Keep me posted on her journey.
Enjoy

Gf

What do I do with my heart?
"This is your Sun Dance"

In 2008 as the Big Short was unfolding, I almost died. I was teaching a class for one of our beloved staff members, who was interviewing to teach in another state where his wife had been offered the job of her lifetime. A multi-aged group of children and I were inside of a stone circle called the medicine wheel. We were noticing how each direction was marked by a pole with a flag on it: a yellow flag for the east, a red flag for the south, a black flag for the west, and a white flag for the north. We sat in the inner circle near a fire pit. I was facing west, the direction of transformation and death, explaining the meaning implied for each direction and pointing to the sky, which I called Grandfather or Tonkashila, and touching the earth and calling it Pachamamita. I lit a small sage bundle and let each child smell it. As the smoke rose, we all watched. I set the sage stick down on a flat rock and failed to notice that it had rolled off into the dry grass starting a small grass fire. The fire began to spread, and the wind picked up. As the fire spread, I told the oldest child, Zack, to get a bucket of water. As he was leaving and I was attempting to put out the fire by stamping on it with my shoes, I told him to take the children back to the school instead. He gathered them, and I continued to try to put out the fire. Alone now as I watched the fire travel much faster than my feeble attempts to put it out, I felt something in my chest. I stopped and watched as the fire spread to the stones and stopped as if it were a perfectly orchestrated controlled burn.

My heart attack did not stop. I didn't know what it was, so I lay down hoping it would let go. It did not. I got up and walked home. I sat in a comfortable chair and called the school asking for Holly. Holly and I had just completed a training in something called the Callahan Technique of Thought Field Therapy.

I wanted her to try the trauma sequence to see if it would help. She came to our house, completed the sequence, and my heart attack let go. I went to a staff meeting.

The next day after having an EKG done by my friend Dr. Harsha I was admitted to a hospital, and by the week's end I had undergone a quadruple heart-bypass operation. My hospital stay was eleven days long, ten days longer than my previous hospital stay. I came home and five weeks later was readmitted with a rare bone infection. Another operation was required, leaving my chest with a huge open wound and a host of doctors, including all three of my brothers, thinking that I was in an uncertain fight for my life.

Between the seventh and eighth week of recovery with an IV in my arm and a huge course of antibiotics in my body, I fell over in a restaurant. I now had a kidney stone. It took six months for this rite of passage to come to some sort of an ending.

During the hospital stays, the long recovery, the endless doctor visits, and test results, I dove inside of myself. I couldn't watch TV or interact with the computer much. I wasn't reading anything or listening to anything. I was on a self-imposed vision quest. I found myself surrendered and content. I knew that my life so far had been filled with miracles and that I needed to make sure in every moment I had left to wake up in gratitude. It would become my new North Star. Awaken and stay awake.

In the hospital I had many visitors, all of whom helped me in nourishing ways. My friend and teacher Jorge Arenivar, who for over twenty years had led our community in the sweat lodge and had guided me on a vision quest, a four-day fast and prayer in the wild, gave me the greatest gift of all. He looked at me lying there in a hospital bed and asked to see my scar. I pulled up my hospital gown, and he said, "Oh Pheeel, this is your Sun Dance!"

I knew enough about the Sun Dance to know that you do it for your community. You dance connected to a tree from first sun until last sun, and at the end you carry a scar from the piercing that connected you to the tree. Jorge gave me a name that transformed my experience from patient to Sun Dancer.

The part about serving the community arose just after our fortieth reunion in the form of a three-word phrase that occurred to me as I walked from our home to school on the wood-chip path that was my commute. "You are done." It was time to transition from my role as the school's director into the unknown.

One of the first things we built during the first year of our school experiment was the teepee that Bruce and Ann Tubbs guided us through to completion. In the 1980s we were chosen by J. C. Eaglesmith, Wallace Black Elk, and Jorge Arenivar to introduce non-indigenous people to the sweat-lodge ceremony. Many people in this area and in our learning community have benefitted greatly by these ceremonies, and some have gone on a vision quest, and some have become Sun Dancers. All of this inner work is intended for us to go out into the world and bring more love and interconnectedness into being.

My childhood friend Glenn Frey died on Martin Luther King's birthday. He was sixty-seven years old, one month younger than me. His song "What Do I Do with My Heart" was the song I worked on to get in touch with my love for him and with my sadness, and it worked. I felt him and his gift, and I discovered the personal and transpersonal message for us all. As a Sun Dancer who was protected by the medicine wheel to survive a heart attack, I especially appreciated these lyrics:

I'll do anything
To save what we had,
I'll love you 'till death do us part.
But what do I do

When I'm still missing you,
What do I do,
What do I do with my heart?

Our Lives as a Series of Rites of Passages

A rite of passage is a creative opportunity to invent ways for children to discover their calling. It is perhaps one of the most powerful parenting tools we have. What if as parents, grandparents, friends, and relatives we reframed much of our gift-giving and some vacations as rites of passages? What if we conspired to align with our children's calling as our top priority as parents, teachers, friends, and relatives? Can we imagine an entire culture bent on discovering our life's purpose? Instead of the tired, outmoded idea that an education is the pathway to our sure success, what if our dreams became the pathway to our salvation? What if we crossed the chasm that Joe Campbell described in the hero's journey and found ourselves living in a world that worked for all of humanity? What if that brave new world was the true stepping stone to a new evolutionary era where fear and scarcity no longer dominate all affairs governed by humans? What if the word *love* became a dance and, as Leonard Cohen wrote, we began to dance to the end of love?

Chapter Six

THE NINE PRINCIPLES OF CHILDHOOD AS SACRED TERRITORY

The trouble with earthlings is their early adulthood. As long as they are young, they are lovable, open-hearted, tolerant, eager to learn and to collaborate. They can even be induced to play with one another. Most adults, however are mortal enemies. The only educational problem Earth has is how to keep them young.

—*Ashley Montagu*

A rite of passage is like a threshold or a portal that takes us into a new realm. It can be, as we have seen, planned or unplanned. It prepares us for the uncertainty of life. My experience at Upland Hills School has shown me that childhood itself is a prolonged rite of passage and something more. For humans, unlike any other species on earth, childhood is an extended passage where maturation occurs slowly and over a longer period of time. The cosmologist Brian Swimme says it this way:

One theory offered by scientists is particularly fascinating. It suggests that humanity had its origin in the prolongation of childhood. The idea is that mutations took place that slowed down our development. Humans went through the same phases as say the chimpanzees, but they remained in each stage for a longer period of time. In particular, this meant that the humans were childlike for more of their lives than other mammals. So to understand what makes a human human, we can study the children of any mammalian species. They jump to play. They explore the world with their eyes, and they taste the world with their mouths. Simple existence thrills them. Their actions are, in some sense, free.

In other words, humanity has evolved to the point it has *because* we have been allowed to develop and experience these childlike traits of play, curiosity, creativity for its own sake, exploration, and wonder. In a certain sense, the technological advances we've made until now, and civilization itself, have their roots in this magical playground called childhood.

And yet this extended childhood, this time of prolonged innocence and discovery, is currently under attack. Today's children, whether they are among the poorest of us or the wealthiest of us, are more vulnerable than at any other time in the history of life on this planet. The poorest children of the world are subjected to all of the worst aspects of our species. They are being starved to death, frightened on the run, used for war, or violently abused. The most privileged are being tested, rated, distracted, overprotected, lied to, confused, labeled, and neglected. In order for our species to navigate this next evolutionary passage where we mature into self-intelligent co-creators, we must actually treat children like the "precious cargo" the bumper sticker implies.

We need to shift our view of childhood as a time to prepare obedient consumers to a time of sacred preparation for each child to become the individual he or she was meant to be. Once we fully understand that every day and every moment of this prolonged childhood is sacred, we will, community by community, wake up into a new world. A world where the sacred territory of childhood is protected, nourished, defended, and honored. A world where each child is embedded in a connected community and supported to develop into a new being—one who honors all life and who is willing to use her talents and skills on behalf of something bigger than herself.

When Ashley Montagu wrote the quote I used to introduce this chapter, we lived in a very different world. It was a world where childhood was being protected much more than it is today. Today's children are both more complicated and more confused. Today's child is more adept yet more crippled. Today's children think fame means success and money is counted in billions. They have access to more information than any society that has ever existed, but they are literally starving for something more.

When the new paradigm is in place and more people understand what is truly valuable, wisdom will replace celebrity. Very early on—beginning with my attraction to and connection with J. Krishnamurti and Buckminster Fuller—I sought out wise elders so I would have a direct experience that might inspire my own development. I cherished the time I would spend alone with that individual, as I appointed myself chauffeur and one-man welcoming committee.

It takes about seventy minutes without traffic to get from our school to the airport. During one such ride, I had beside me someone who was telling me a story about meeting Albert Einstein. He was describing Einstein's house in exquisite detail and a moment when he was waiting on the front porch by a screen door when he heard violin music drifting out into that particular summer's day. By the time my passenger got to the part where he was shaking hands with the wild-haired scientist, I was right there with him.

My drive with the brilliant anthropologist Ashley Montagu came when I had just begun to appreciate childhood as sacred territory. I had read his book *Growing Young* and was inspired by his theory of "neoteny"—cultivating and sustaining child-like traits like curiosity and play throughout our entire lifetime. His enthralling storytelling told me he most definitely practiced what he had been preaching.

It was one of those times when you drive more than an hour so absorbed in a story or conversation that you can't recall anything about the drive itself. It was as if time vanished, and his story, the tone of his voice, his faint English accent, and his eloquence captivated my entire being. He had been invited as our featured guest at an event that we called "Project School House." It was 1987, and our school was going through its own rite of passage as we faced the challenge of keeping the school going during a recession and time of low enrollment. We noticed we had begun to doubt our mission and our ability to attract enough students to move forward.

We realized we needed to take a proactive step forward, and Project School House was the vehicle for hitting re-start. We drew up plans and made a model of a new school building to represent that new beginning. We had learned from our past experiences that when we set an intention to build something, it served as a metaphor for something more. Project School House would be our first capital campaign. We were ready to share our vision with as many people who would listen, and we were gearing up the courage to ask for the time, talent, and treasure to support that vision.

When it came time to structure an event that would bring us together and set the stage for requesting financial support, we talked about whom might we ask to anchor the evening. A parent from our school had given me a book, and I had shared it with several staff members. Its message was in perfect harmony for the moment. *Growing Young* was the title of the book, and its author was the man sitting next to me.

Ashley Montagu, like Bucky, was an integrator and a generalist. An anthropologist who made major contributions to nearly every social movement of the last seventy years, Ashley was a living example of someone who was always "growing young" and his presence in the life of our school was pivotal.

After he returned home, we shared a correspondence that introduced me to the leading edge of brain science, evolutionary theories, child development, and evolutionary thinker Pierre Teilhard de Chardin. He sent me articles, small books, and inspirational notes from his home in Princeton, New Jersey. In one of those notes he wrote,

"What a privilege it is to be a teacher, one of the unacknowledged legislators of the world—and therefore the least rewarded by even a scintilla of recognition, anyway, however pessimistic one may at times be, the only philosophically tenable position in a time of crisis for a pessimist is optimism—to work as if by our labor we will make a difference. —Stay well, with lots of love and fond memories of the school and you."

It was Ashley who gave me the scientific evidence and the living example of how and why childhood must be defended as sacred territory. In the aforementioned book *Growing Young* he writes about the child as being the forerunner of humanity and of childhood as being the foundational period of our lives and therefore our species. The process of growing young—neoteny—involves retaining and cultivating key traits well into adulthood. These traits, if developed and nourished during our sacred childhoods, help to insure that some or most of them stay with us our entire lives.

As we were saying goodbye at the airport, I watched this eighty-two-year-young man bound out of the car, gather his suitcase with a flourish, turn with a teary smile, and blow a kiss as he rushed off to his gate. During that one hour car ride, I experienced these traits of neoteny from our guest: friendship, sensitivity, the need to think soundly, curiosity, playfulness, a sense of wonder, creativity, open-mindedness, resiliency, a sense of humor, joyfulness, laughter and tears, honesty and trust, and compassionate intelligence.

We now know why we have to make sacred this time we call childhood. The fate of our species rests on doing just this. And . . . this is something children cannot do for themselves. They need the nurturance, protection, and encouragement from the adults who are closest to them. Yes, teachers of course. And even more so, parents. Meaning we must recognize parenthood as a sacred rite of passage as well. For our puppies, mama-hood is over in less than a year—age seven in dog years. For we humans—and every parent reading this will attest to it—the passage lasts twenty years, thirty years, and sometimes a lifetime. Parenthood is extended to grand-parenthood and if we are truly fortunate, great-grandparenthood. At the very least, the period where the hands-on work is done and the most presence is required is eighteen years.

Much has changed since I was a youngster fifty or sixty years ago. It was the era of the stay-at-home mom, sending dad off to work with a lunch pail, and kids with their lunchboxes. After school, children had more timeless time—and yet never too far from a watchful eye. Since then we have families where two parents are working and broken families where one member is gone. Children are left to institutional childcare and electronic baby-sitters. Like the classic Harry Chapin song of more than forty years ago, "Cat's in the Cradle," absent and indifferent parents miss the child's growing up—and the child follows the model to become an "absent" adult.

This is not said to shame or blame parents who are dealing with the economic challenges of post-industrial society. However it *is* to remind them that they have a choice, and how they choose will impact not just the future of their children, but the future of all children.

Before we go deeper into how to protect the sacred territory of childhood, perhaps we should first clarify what we mean by *sacred*, a word with religious connotations. Beyond religious rituals, shrines, and symbols, the word *sacred* implies something so important that it is worthy of awe, reverence, and deep respect. When something is deemed sacred, it is inferred that it requires special treatment and special protection. As I suggested earlier, despite great advances in standard of living and quality of life, childhood is perhaps less sacred—less respected, revered, and protected—than it was when I was a child.

This has happened almost imperceptibly, as the pace of life has sped up and leisure time has become a lot less leisurely, at least in the United States. Well-meaning parents who want their children to have successful lives—which means, more and more, financial success—often march their too-young children into premature testing and academic preparation, skipping some of those key passages that Jean Piaget identified. This has compressed childhood into a series of activities—even "play" activities like sports, dance, the martial arts—to the point where children have no time for childhood.

Another result of focusing primarily on the material world and material success is that the emphasis is what integral philosopher Ken Wilber calls the "it" and "its" quadrants—the external manifestations that become the markers of success in our society. The more internal qualities—curiosity, imagination, intuition, and indeed the "self-intelligence" Krishnamurti talked about—are too often ignored. In Michael Moore's recent film *Where to Invade Next*, he interviews European teachers who are incredulous that many American schools have dropped the arts because they've been deemed "not relevant" to future achievement.

So when I say childhood is sacred territory, I mean that school-age children not only need to be protected in terms of physical safety, their inner world and development require protection too. Their playtime, curiosity, exploration, and imagination require the same awe, reverence, and respect as the academic subjects, which are of course important too. And . . . none of these achievements can define who a child truly is. Their one-of-a-kindness, their unique genius, and their flaws; this is sacred too, perhaps the most sacred thing of all.

My mom, bless her, hit the Jewish-mother trifecta. Three of her four sons grew up to be medical doctors. This had nothing to do with imposing her idea of success on them and everything to do with creating the sacred space for them to be themselves and follow their own guiding star—the same thing that allowed me to do what I have done in my own career. I was fortunate to have had parents who intrinsically understood the sacred nature of childhood. All I want is for every child to have that same opportunity, and that's what the rest of this chapter is about.

The 9 Guidelines

Based on our own forty-plus years of experience in recognizing what children need to thrive and the key qualities that will serve them and their world their whole life through, I've come up with nine guidelines that protect and nourish the sacred territory of childhood. Together, these guidelines create and hold the space for childhood to unfold in a way that will allow children to develop the trust, confidence, and agility that they will need to navigate the world as it is and co-create the one we've never seen.

1. Live Love
2. Sky Time
3. Somatic Awareness
4. Safety and Trust
5. Feed the Right Brain
6. Exercise the Left Brain
7. Generate Esteem
8. Adventure
9. Community

Guideline I
Live Love

The trees are blowing on Valentine's Day.
Snow is still.
Love is spreading all over the world.

— *Velvet*

I can't define love. Perhaps no one can, and that's why our artists continually and creatively attempt to. Living love is an aspiration. It's our collective attempt to put into practice, feeling, and communicating our deep underlying inter-connectivity. When we live and practice love, we feel deeply connected to each other and to this world we belong to. One of the first conditions of living love is the ability to receive it. We can take our cue from evolution's design and imagine the first nourishing of a baby at its mother's breast. The contentment of being loved, the warmth of touch, cheek on breast, and the complete nourishment of mother's milk are all hints on how to live love.

Love is so fundamental to who we are—and who we become—that it is the first quality of sacred childhood. Children need to be loved, to feel loved, and see this love expressed by and through the adults around them. Being and feeling loved is how children first feel like they "belong." First they belong to a mother, then to a family, then to all relatives and their friends, and then to a group or village. In our global contemporary culture, schools provide our first dynamic group interaction beyond our inner circle. If a school aspires to practice love, then it must be a place where children feel connected—with the adults caring for them, with the other children, with the world itself, and the web of life.

To widen the circle of belongingness to the school community means a deep rapport must be established between teacher and child the very first day of school. This rapport—a combination of love, caring, and mutual trust—is what first creates the sacred space where a child can be free to discover the world and who they are in it. It provides the safety to take the important risks that are part of development.

The youngest group at our school usually consists of between ten and twelve children. It is, by design, the smallest adult-to-child ratio. The primary reason for this is to help all of the children form a bond to each other and to their teacher. This rapport is the promise and proof that they do belong, and it creates a deep trust. Over the past four decades we have seen firsthand how children are changing and evolving. Our frantic, distracted, materialistic, complex, and perplexing culture has delivered a wide range of children to our door. One of the first markers of "living love" in our youngest group is the development of friendship, and it doesn't seem to matter whether two friends are similar or wildly different.

Friendship that develops outside of the family is one of life's most precious miracles and is itself a key passage as children learn living love. This neotenous trait occurring between children who are four through seven is the pot of gold at the end of a rainbow. How it happens and why it happens between any particular two children is a mystery. When it does happen, as in the case of Lucy and Lauren, it radiates an energy that flows into the school and into the homes of each child. There is an enchantment that occurs when two souls meet and connect, and in many instances it lasts a lifetime.

Lucy is an active, engaging child who loves being front and center. She dances, sings, acts, inquires, and needs to know what's going on in every room. Lauren is thoughtful, open, kind, and curiously mindful. She pauses sometimes to find the right word, and she uses words with care and empathy. At first glance we might oversimplify as "opposites attract," but we humans are complex, and as I said earlier there is a mystery of relatedness that transcends the obvious.

These two girls delight in each other's company and have learned how to navigate disputes, differences, even time and distance so that they can be together. The mystical reason is that when they are together they mutually enter into a timeless state. While talking with Lauren's mother, I discovered that when they get together at her house the same pattern emerges over and over again. They go into a room and discuss the guidelines for their play. There's an openness and excitement between them that allows each to be leader and contributor. They then enter into their agreement and pass through an invisible portal where they lose time and travel wherever their imaginations take them.

Play, too, is the sacred territory of childhood. This is the part of our childhood that takes advantage of our open minds when real and unreal merge and blend. From the invisible playmate to the invention of a new town called Woodville, it lives outside of time and logic, another quality of the sacred.

The trust and the mutual creative excitement that arise out of being together create a form of enlightenment. The ingredients are not as important as the ability to repeat this time after time. Once we have experienced this ability to mutually awaken, we always remember it. It is an experience of no worry. It is something that we can keep alive for our entire lifetime if we nurture it. It is a gift that lives beyond time and space, has no wrapping paper, takes up no space, and will never need to be returned. This gift is the gift of a sacred childhood, and its value lives longer than any toy, game, screen, or amusement-park experience.

Living love and teaching from it as a source creates the safety, protection, and enchantment that allow children to develop imagination and fantasy. These are the keys to becoming visionaries of a new future.

Guideline II
Make Time for "Sky Time"

I have often heard my fellow educators talk about the amount of "seat time" required to teach a given subject, thereby equating seat time with learning. To counterbalance the "unnatural world" of sitting quietly in a seat listening, children need to experience the natural world, the world outdoors. "Sky time" is what we call the time children spend in nature and outdoors with each other, and it's one of the best ways to help the human brain grow. The natural world provides the complexity and depth, the variety and the challenges that foster rapid and intricate new neural pathways in brain development.

Some of our greatest educational "work" comes outdoors on the "playing field." Consider that outdoor playtime helps children make their own decisions, become leaders (and when appropriate, followers). They invent—and "out-vent." That is, they release lots of pent-up energy so that when the time comes for focus and concentration indoors, that comes as naturally as playing outside. Thus sky time is the perfect environment for optimal brain development.

Children who fall in love with the natural world will protect, defend, nourish, and nurture it. They will feel as if they belong in nature and will grow into adults who value the systems that support all of life on this spaceship we call Earth. Honoring and venerating the natural world as a primary teacher is a way of living love. When we consider nature in this way, she becomes another mother. This is why we hear people in so many languages speak about our "mother earth."

We have a dress code at our school: dress for the weather. I have often looked outside my window to see our children playing in the worst possible weather conditions. I have seen them sliding on ice while 33-degree rain was falling. I have seen them covered in mud. I have seen them outside when the temperature was below zero and they had to be called in. I have seen them play "all-school games" for an hour on a frozen, snow-covered field while north arctic winds blew. The biggest adjustment our kids have to make when they graduate from eighth grade is having to spend so much "seat time" bound by four walls and a roof.

One of our former students has devoted over nineteen years (and still counting) to our National Park Service, first in Denali and currently in Yosemite. When Jesse was a child at our school, I'd often notice him at the edges of the pond. He loved watching life emerge, and he loved sharing his excitement with his classmates and teachers. As a young adult, he took an interest in our community sweat lodges, and it was during one of those lodges where I heard him pray.

I remember how his prayer touched my heart. I was listening to someone who I knew from the early age of five and had grown into a lover of the natural world. This was before he received a bachelor's degree in psychology from the University of Michigan and a graduate certificate from the Leadership for Public Lands and Cultural Heritage program; this was his soul sharing his deep connection with earth and sky, and as his former teacher I found it more powerful than any college diploma or degree.

He is currently the director of the UC Merced Wilderness Education Center. His love of the natural world and being out under the sky have been translated into developing a graduate-level education program designed to develop the next generation of national park leaders. His passions and his interests are now shaping a new generation of leaders.

Thanks to his loving parents, who encouraged and supported his love of the natural world through backpacking and camping trips, Jesse is now a teacher of teachers. He and his sister Naomi both work and serve in Yosemite. They have chosen to live their lives outside, under the stars and the vast California sky. They have been drawn to this by their deep connection with the great outdoors. This cannot be taught in a classroom. It happens when you are young and the world outside the rooms of your home are calling you, calling you to come, come discover the practice of the wild.

In our human history, the sky was the first television screen. The stars, the moon, the planets, and the Milky Way were the screen upon which our first ancestors imagined and learned from. The night sky still enchants if we allow it to, and time under the sky is a key ingredient for children. Instead of learning how to navigate the vast oceans as our first sea captains did, the children of this time and the future will need vast amounts of sky time to navigate a future that will honor all of the systems that nourish and support life on this sacred planet.

Guideline III
Cultivate Somatic Awareness

We believe our body has its own intelligence, a wisdom that cuts through the mind games that often dominate our choices. In our quest to protect the sacred territory of childhood, we must be models for our children, and we must search for skillful ways of communicating with them. We could teach them about the art of listening to our inner wisdom. If there's one thing I've learned about human behavior, it is that you can only change you. Which is why as parents our ultimate influence will be as models for our children. If we say one thing and do the other, we can be sure that our children will only notice what we do and discount what we say.

A key to being and teaching congruence is cultivating body awareness and somatic intelligence. So how do we learn to listen to our body's intelligence? One way is by learning how to be still. We practice stillness daily. We learn how to listen beneath the surface, and if we listen carefully enough, our body tells us what it wants and needs for nourishment.

We all need food to live, and in the current "foodie" culture, we often have too many choices as to what we eat. It's easy to give in to external pulls, which makes it more important to listen inside for the cues from "somatic intelligence." Our work with children over four decades has led me to these basic guidelines: eat organic fruit and vegetables, limit processed foods, limit sugar, eat whole grains, eat locally and in season, and be flexible and loving with yourself and your children as you celebrate eating meals together.

When we come to a meal, as a family or as a community, we have the option of saying grace. While this can be construed as a religious ritual, gratitude has no religion. And . . . it's a sacred practice. Whatever it is we *do* eat takes on an extra glow and extra dimension when we pause to be grateful. That pause to reflect on the web of life and human endeavor that has brought this food to our table slows us down in a world that seems to be constantly speeding up. Think about it. How often do we eat in a hurry, driving or talking on our smart phones? The moment of stillness, peace, and gratitude prepares our body to eat. We may even eat more slowly and eat less food. And enjoy the meal more.

Somatic awareness simply means that you have learned how to treat your body as a sacred vessel. Parents who want their children to grow into healthy, vibrant, vital adults will consider practicing and modeling good eating habits, regular exercise, proactive health care, and mindfulness in our choice of words and actions.

One of our former students, Ruth, practices the art of Ayurvedic medicine. This five-thousand-year-old practice from India is in wide use today because of its emphasis on balance. When I was recovering from my heart attack, I reconnected with Ruth and experienced her integrated approach to my situation as she offered reading materials (e.g., *The Omnivore's Dilemma*), specific advice about oils and their medicinal uses, as well as guidance on specific types of acupuncture and massage. Her holistic approach hastened my recovery and gave me access to my inner healer.

In our school there is a community-supported agriculture plot within walking distance from our school. Because of our Michigan climate we use this garden mostly in the fall. Every week for the first ten weeks of school, children have the opportunity to attend a class that harvests the food for that week and the next day prepares enough food for the entire school to eat. This simple class broadens every student's palate by presenting fresh organic food grown locally and offered in the afternoon when the children are most hungry.

Whenever you or your child gets sick, you have an opportunity to use it as a lesson. We are vulnerable when we're sick and in some ways open to learning about how not to get sick again. Conversations and actions at this time might lead to a greater awareness of how miraculous our bodies are and how sensitive they are to particular things. As a parent you can help the child by keeping an inventory of specific aspects of their health and as they grow empower them to take over that function.

Guideline IV
Create Safety and Trust

Because we're using love as our true north, safety takes on many meanings. It can of course mean physical safety—it is most important to physically protect the children in our charge from real danger. There is emotional safety as well, so children are willing to risk making a mistake without being ridiculed or diminished. As we've seen, the various rites of passage of childhood involve taking a series of risks, of venturing into unfamiliar territory. Like a toddler learning to walk looks back at his or her parents for reassurance, children need a fundamental sense of safety in order to navigate new experiences. They need the reassurance "We have your back."

Perhaps the most clarifying expression of "risk inside the context of safety" is what we call the "trust fall" where children have the opportunity to fall backward off a platform and then be "caught" by the rest of the children. It feels terribly risky to fall backward without looking—and in this case, it is completely safe. Every child who has tried has successfully fallen, and none have been injured. We want children to know "We've got you." It is safe to fall back into the arms of the Universe.

During this sacred time when children develop confidence by testing themselves in the world, we create safety through the words we choose and the way we communicate with children in relation to risk and danger, self-esteem, and clear personal boundaries. It's our job as parents and teachers to create many opportunities where our children learn how to take risks within a safe container. The way we encourage them to do this is to use our words consciously and carefully. We say things that support them while giving them the opportunity to opt out without feeling failure or shame. Our goal is to empower, and the best way to empower is to let them decide when to jump. Literally.

Our school installed an adventure playground in the late 1980s. An adventure playground is a ropes course with low and high "elements" that are designed to challenge the children and reward risk. Each of the elements has a name and presents a specific type of challenge. The Kitten Crawl invites two people to walk on taut airplane cables that form the letter V. The only way to do this successfully is to interlock your hands to your partner's hands facing each other and leaning in to each other with complete trust, until you both reach the perch at the end of the cable. This element teaches trust, balance, strategy, and co-operation. Every child that uses the course is between nine and fourteen years old. Each wears safety gear that is specifically designed for that element. The pièce de résistance of the course is the zip line located twenty feet above the ground between two large trees about 150 feet apart. This offers a direct experience of flight.

We train students who support and assist with the zip line—one who positions himself at the head of Burma Bridge (three cables stretched between two trees with a safety line overhead) and the other on the platform where the zipper prepares to take off. Both of these students have zipped themselves and have calm, compassionate demeanors. They are leaders in this class, and the children respect and trust them. When the prospective "zipper" is on the platform and all safety devices are secure, the teacher on the ground goes through a checklist of all safety connections. This simple procedure reminds everyone that the safety of the child is paramount. We only allow positive comments, and there are times when a student on the ground might say, "Oh, don't be a chicken," and that student is warned or told to leave the class. This enforces the atmosphere of empowerment, and only when the prospective zipper puts their thumbs up does the countdown begin. If the student does not want to zip or is frozen on the platform, they are gently encouraged to go back the way they came, and they are acknowledged for getting to the platform in the first place.

There is nothing like watching a child zip for the first time. They take that leap from the platform as one person, and they come back as another. They radiate the confidence that comes with facing their fears and learning to trust. No grade, gold stars, or team points are needed. Experiencing their own courage is their reward.

Ian's father was the founder of the Waldorf Institute, a teacher-training center that was located in Southfield, Michigan. He was a brilliant educator and my mentor for the years his son attended our school. Ian was unhappy at the local Waldorf school, and so his mother and father sought us out. His father was a wise soul who knew his son quite well and made the decision to place him in our school based on what he and his wife felt were Ian's best interests. Ian loved anything that moved, including the internal-combustion engine, which was a bit of an irony since his father didn't even drive a car. Ian was very physical; he loved to play and loved challenging himself. His father was a gifted teacher who believed that schools evolve and need to integrate all of their parts into a cohesive whole.

When Ian came to our school, he was eleven years old, and he immediately took to the adventure playground. He excelled as a teacher and as an agile participant. He zipped the first time out. He taught others how to strategize and how to overcome their fears. He led by example and always placed others before himself. He was one of those special leaders who took great delight in someone else's success. The course was a metaphor for all that he had hungered for. Choice, challenge, collaboration, character, and creativity were all values that Ian demonstrated and embodied.

His father was in his mid-fifties when Ian was enrolled. We spent long hours together whenever he visited our school, and I learned about the autonomous nature of how Waldorf schools grow and develop. He encouraged me to use wherever we were, the geographical place, as a primary teacher. I understood what he meant after watching how each child hugged the trees of the adventure playground as they passed from one element to the next. His son graduated from our school a happy, confident leader, quite the opposite of the sullen, deflated boy he was when we first met.

I traveled to New York state to visit Ian's father a few days before he died. Entering a dark room and noticing how frail he was, I was surprised when his eyes lit up. He offered me his hand, and I thanked him for all that he had given me. His huge eyebrows perked up, and he asked me to lean closer to his face. I noticed how alive he seemed in that moment and how present and unafraid he was. He said he was sorry. I asked him why. He said he had intended to write one more book before he died. That book was to be entitled *Schools that Work*, and he looked into the distance and told me that our school was going to be in that book.

His son Ian never adjusted to schools. He resented being judged and made to play a game that made no sense to him. He was drawn to rock climbing, a sport that forces one to attempt the impossible and calls forth tactical thinking. He loved to try hard for no reason. He became a part of an international community that followed the warm weather so that they could continue to go where no one else would ever dare. They formed a bond around defining success and fulfillment on their own terms.

After a near-death motocross accident, Ian began his own self-education by reading and learning new skills like computer-aided design (CAD). As the CEO of his own company, ID Sculpture, he is bringing rock climbing to children and adults through innovative playground structures that challenge within the context of safety first. I think of Ian on a sheer cliff, laser-focused, inventing new handholds as he solves the challenge before him. He has learned to take one step at a time, to be totally present, to remain calm in the face of danger, and to make possible the impossible. Summiting a cantilevered ledge is a form of meditation, a transcendent practice that requires courage and risk. But behind the risk there are redundant safety measures that reinforce how important it is to emphasize not just the risk but also the sometimes-invisible safety nets that allow us to risk. This mindfulness is another way that we as adults support childhood as sacred territory.

Ian's courageous story was in a way made possible by his parents' courage to find a school that worked for their son. It took them over a year to find us, but they were determined. It took courage for Ian to put himself back together after his accident. It takes courage to invent your own company without any academic credentials and accept the role you created for yourself. It takes courage to become a father of a five-year-old daughter who is already skiing faster than any other little kid on the mountain. It takes courage to attempt to live in a world where everything is changing and yet to be mindful of the dangers just ahead. The sacred territory of childhood must include the courage to let our children become who they were meant to be, as safely as possible, and then to let them go. It takes courage to love.

Guideline V
Feed the Right Brain

Knowledge is not rooted in facts; it's rooted in curiosity.

The right hemisphere of our brain is where our creative, artistic, and musical talents reside. If as parents we model a lifelong drive to improve and grow and if we live lives of adventure and are open to learning new things, we are modeling the traits that improve our amazing brains. I've read that the liver and kidney we are born with will be very much the same when we die, but our brain is the only organ that can literally evolve. Every time we learn a new song, or play a new game, or seek out new ideas, or adventure into the unknown we are modeling for our children lives rich in creativity and curiosity.

Children, unlike adults, are eager to exercise this part of their brains. They gravitate to art, music, poetry, theatre, clay, and building as if these were the most engaging and important things in the entire world. What we've learned over these years is that the creative and performing arts are the essential center of our curriculum and that language, math, and science, when taught creatively, are vastly improved when the right brain is engaged.

Cultivating this kind of curiosity and spontaneity doesn't necessarily "look" as good as it sounds, meaning that a school that is based on love is full of messes. Creativity is a messy process. Right-brain food is open-ended, surprising, fun, engaging, engrossing, musical, frustrating, challenging, and alive. When you as a parent share your love of music or art, you are feeding right-brain food to your child.

The creative and performing arts contain within them their own deep rewards. A child who has written a poem from their heart has already received a gift. If their teacher likes it and lets the child know, another gift is given, and if that child reads it to her class, the gift is once again passed along. Our current popular culture is transfixed on making the performing arts a place where there is one winner and many losers. This contamination distorts the true beauty of performing as a singer or an actor. One of the most valuable aspects of the performing arts is its emphasis on collaboration. True collaboration is not about winning; it's about artistic synergy. The experience of being in a play can transform a shy child into a confident one, all the while teaching the importance of collaboration.

Patrick came to us at the age of seven. He was a shy, affable child who liked to watch from the sidelines. During the winter trimester of his first year, he joined the guitar class. His teacher Ted had inherited the class from me. Our intention was to introduce the guitar to children of all ages and to pray that by the end of an hour we were finally in tune and still sane.

Patrick was entranced by his borrowed instrument, and by the time he was eight, he was playing well enough for his parents to buy him his first guitar. It was just after receiving his guitar that his entire class merged together as one while playing the Beatles song "Here Comes the Sun," and he was hooked. Ted asked him to join the band that played for our spring musical. He watched from the pit for three years before he decided he might like to be in a play. He had noticed that in Ted and Karen he had found teachers who honored the theatre with deep respect, yet at the same time they made sure that every kid felt safe to drop a line or forget a direction. The bottom line with both of the teachers was that you try your hardest and you learn to collaborate for the greater good.

In the play *Three Strong Women* Ted had written a song entitled "I Wish I Could Fly Away," a beautiful ballad sung by a father to his daughter about letting go. The play was set in

Japan and was taken from a Japanese folk tale that was turned into a children's book by Rafe Martin and given to Karen so that she could turn it into a musical. When Patrick, dressed in a kimono, began to sing, the entire audience fell into a profound silence. I remember shedding tears. The die was cast.

This shy introvert was encouraged by his parents and by his teachers to take the risk and reveal his gift. He never looked back. Now twenty-five, he is an equity actor who is making a living in Chicago. His peak experience as an adult was performing the lead role in *Spring Awakening*. He has devoted his life to his calling. The play opened in Chicago to rave reviews— which seemed to impress everyone but Pat. He recently realized that he did his best when he paid very little attention to the critics and devoted his performance to his fellow actors and his director. For twenty performances of *Spring Awakening* his life was that perfect meld of hard work, collaboration, artistic expression, and creativity—and it paid the rent.

He has met actors in Chicago who began working when they were children and consequently were in some ways deprived of childhood because of their narrow focus on acting. Pat feels that the right-brain food that he was offered at Upland Hills gave him much more. His love of the guitar has only enhanced his career because an actor who can play an instrument is in greater demand. As for his sacred childhood, he has vivid memories of tracking animals, star gazing, launching rockets, and playing all-school games on a mud-soaked field, all of which contribute to his deep love and respect for parents who encouraged him to go beyond their world of "get a degree and a good job that pays well."

The right-brain food of his sacred childhood is still feeding not just Pat, but his family, his friends, his community, and audiences in the city of Chicago. When he took the risk of stepping out on stage and singing in his sweet, kind, and tender voice the lyrics of "I Wish I Could Fly Away," he found his true essence. He flew away from that shy, inhibited boy because of us. He was meant to perform in service of a story, live and on stage in front of real people who were there to be moved. In his heart he knows that it was his teachers who made it all possible, his teachers and his school community who loved, protected, and nourished him so he could fly away.

Guideline VI
Exercise the Left Brain

In order for children to grow into the people that they were meant to be, they must learn about and cultivate the power of intention. When we use our left brain to set an intention, we take charge of our own destiny. This is why it's so important for children to begin making their own decisions at an early age. Our school culture is deliberately designed for children to make choices and for them to follow through with the choices they make. When we use our brains in this way on a daily basis, we strengthen our ability to discern and to deepen.

Left-brain exercise is goal oriented. We decide we want to build a box, and then we try to build one. We make lists of things we want to accomplish, and then we check them off one by one. Many schools make these lists for us. In fact, the curricula that dominate school cultures consist of giant lists of the subjects you need to learn, and then each subject has a subset of more things you need to learn. These externally imposed lists and standards drain the joy out of learning. In a school dedicated to every student realizing their potential, a different approach emerges that is as natural as inhaling and exhaling. The "inhale" is when a child is offered options and directions; the "exhale" is when they make a choice. Thus, the school day becomes a rich mix of independence and inter-dependence, of being a leader and being a learner, of guiding and being guided.

In our school culture, the ultimate experience of seeing an endeavor through from vision, through intention, to manifestation is the senior project, reserved for the oldest students. The process begins with the student deciding on some endeavor that will have lasting value for them and for their community. Some of our students begin thinking about their senior project when they're quite young, while most begin in earnest at the very onset of their eighth-grade year. Their teacher creates the scaffolding for them to organize their ideas, brainstorm with the group, and eventually pitch the idea before the entire staff at the opening of our Wednesday staff meeting.

Isaac presented his idea of building an electric guitar at a recent staff meeting. He told us there was a fallen cherry tree in the monastery forest, and he wanted to use that wood for the base of his guitar. He went on to describe how his keen interest in music led him to want to learn how to work with tuning pegs, strings, electronics, native hardwood, and sound. Once he finished the guitar, he thought that offering it as an auction item for our school's auction would be a perfect way to thank his community for all we had given him. It was an awe-inspiring presentation.

Even more impressive was how methodically and carefully he worked through each of the steps that would lead to a successful outcome. His mentor and his father both helped to guide him, but Isaac was clearly leading this effort. He ran into one obstacle after another and each time persevered—right up to the day before the auction when final adjustments had to be made.

On the evening of our auction he got up in front of the entire room of nearly three hundred people. Holding his guitar, he explained how difficult it was to make an electric guitar, especially aligning the neck with the body. He sat down, plugged in his guitar, and played the introduction to "Blackbird." The audience was speechless and the bidding exuberant. When his guitar sold for almost $1,500, a huge cheer went up from the audience. Then he noticed who the buyer was, the father of one of his closest friends.

We now know that brain size has nothing to do with intelligence. What matters is how we use our brains. Brain science has discovered that we can form new axons and dendrites right up until the last years of our lives. If we hold an intention to greet each new day as an adventure, if we are determined to change our bad habits and to take on new challenges, we will be able to live a quality of life filled with happiness. These patterns begin when we set our intentions early on and practice manifesting the electric guitars that are born first as an intention.

Guideline VII
Generate Esteem

In the sacred territory of childhood, it is essential that children learn to unconditionally value themselves. That is, they love and appreciate themselves for who they are and not necessarily for what they do or how well they perform, or conform to the expectations of others. Yes, boundaries must be set so that children learn how to stand for themselves and not encroach on others. At the same time, the sacred space of a child's unique individuality must be respected, protected, and encouraged. Bottom line—a child must feel good about themselves just because. No reason, no performance standard is necessary.

It's understandable that in a society that places so much emphasis on the "it" and "its" quadrants or spheres of life (how things appear from the outside) there's some confusion between self-image and self-esteem. Here is a distinction that has worked for me and worked for us at the school: Self-image is determined by what other people think of us, while self-esteem is born out of how we think of ourselves. So it is this self-esteem that we seek to cultivate.

In order to create an atmosphere where children can build and develop their self-esteem, it is necessary to develop deep, lasting, and forgiving loving-kindness. This practice begins first with ourselves as adults and teachers, and it thrives in an environment that is accepting and welcoming. Self-esteem is often at risk in traditional educational systems. These systems are based on the idea that students are in competition with one another and that to win means to do better than everyone else. Whether it's a test or a paper, a speech or an art project, "education as usual" tends to grade through comparison with others, and there are winners and losers. (Interestingly, the original meaning of the word *competition* in Greek meant to "strive together." Thus when those Greek athletes were "competing" in the Olympics, they really weren't "running against" any other athlete, but instead using that athlete's performance to bring out their own "personal best.")

At the foundation of self-esteem is kindness. That's why we don't allow taunting at our adventure playground. We recognize that each child is competing with him- or herself, and no one else. We encourage risk-taking in the context of kindness. When the child herself decides to "zip," there is complete ownership of that choice. She has exceeded her past personal best—which was getting up there in the first place. And since there is no competition one against the other, everyone else is rooting for her.

Being kind to yourself and to others takes courage. You need to be able to embrace all sides of yourself, the areas where you feel comfortable and the areas that reveal your weaknesses. It's not about good and bad, but more about what helps and what hurts. A child who is deeply loved and has not been conditioned by external demands and judgments feels secure in her skin. She walks into her day with a quiet confidence and shares her love with great sensitivity and generosity. Our job with such a child is to let her know that we see her and that we will protect her compassion for others and always return her love.

For parents and children who are so dependent on others for approval, we can only listen deeply and reflect our deep acceptance for who they are, as we secretly invite them to let go of their suffering. Choosing and creating communities that support and encourage, that care for the earth and each other, that embrace the darkest parts of ourselves while working to change is a key to building and re-building the self-esteem engine.

Nia is an eight-year-old girl who beautifully represents full self-esteem. She smiles often and always looks straight into your eyes. Her words are few but always carefully chosen. She notices when others are agitated and tries to invent ways of soothing them. She uses her free time to explore and is as comfortable with boys as she is with girls. Nia often confides in her teacher, telling her what she's thinking and looking for guidance. Every person in her group knows that they can trust her.

Our school celebrates Martin Luther King Jr.'s birthday. We use it as an opportunity to teach the values and lessons of his remarkable life. Often students who have graduated from our school visit us on that day. Nia came into school that day a bit late, and during her first fresh-air break she approached her teacher with an air of sadness. Her teacher asked her what was wrong, and Nia said that her father, mother, and sister were all home and that she didn't really want to be at school. She wondered why we were here. Her teacher told her that there would be two all-school meetings to celebrate Dr. King's birthday and that perhaps she'd learn something and enjoy how different the day was going to be.

When the day was coming to a close, Nia came up to her teacher with a huge smile and said that even though she didn't want to be at school, she figured since she was there she knew there must be a reason. Now she knew what that reason was. She said that the song "We Shall Overcome" was so beautiful and that she had never heard it before. Then she said when the whole school was invited on the stage to dance to Stevie Wonder's song "Happy Birthday," it was like the whole world filled with love. She left that day feeling joyous and grateful that she had come to school. She experienced a connection to Dr. King's day that truly made it a holy day. A sacred day.

Guideline VIII
Make Every Day an Adventure

Children love an adventure. It can be a simple picnic or a short bike trip, but taken as an adventure, magic and surprise are added. That's why a key guideline for sacred childhood is to make every day an adventure. The word *adventure* implies something unusual is going to happen. So when we greet every day with our children as if something new or magical is in store, childhood becomes unforgettable and forever accessible. That is why we created a school that is full of choices and direct sensory experiences.

Parents who use the word <u>adventure</u> when they are rolling down the driveway are offering an invitation to make an ordinary experience extraordinary. It doesn't matter if it's a trip to the grocery store or a trip to the dentist; the words you use can make this simple trip an adventure. This mindset changes our approach to life in a profound way. When we language life as an adventure, then we begin to notice all the ways life *actually is* an adventure.

Our youngest group at school this year was a challenge for our new teacher and for the school as a whole. I heard something going on outside my office window, and when I looked I noticed my intervention was needed. I discovered eight four-year-olds bickering about sharing the two swings on the swing set while their teacher was off working with three other children. That's when I remembered an earth balloon that I had in my office.

When I returned I told the kids we were going to play a game called "pachamamita." I had no idea of what I was going to do, but this is how adventures are born. I started to blow the balloon up and asked the kids if they knew where we lived on this balloon; with each breath their attention grew. When it was fully inflated, I pointed out Michigan and North America and talked about the Earth as a spaceship. I then asked them to count backwards from ten, and when we got to zero I released the balloon, and it launched, flew, sputtered, and fell to the ground. By now I had their full attention. So I told them that if someone could catch the balloon before it reached the earth I'd give them a winning number. Over and over we launched the balloon with cheers of delight as I provided more and more information about the continents and other earth facts. This invented game became so popular that for days afterwards those children asked if we could play pachamamita.

An adventure is an invitation to go some place, a physical place or an imaginary one. Having the frame "adventure" can make the most ordinary chore or errand extraordinary. It calls forth expectation and anticipation, and it awakens children (and ourselves) to see the old anew. That's what was so enchanting about my ride with Ashley Montagu. He recounted his meeting with Albert Einstein as an adventure and treated our ride to the airport the same way. That's why it became memorable to both of us.

Guideline IX
Circle Up in Community

The children of the future will be called upon to collaborate like no generation before. The environmental, economic, political, and personal issues that face a world in transition from the old paradigm to the new can only be solved in the context of cooperation and community. That's why the sacred territory of childhood must be informed and nourished by community.

Our last guideline involves community circles, so we can become a part of something greater than our family and friends. It points us towards our need to keep expanding our hearts and make our exclusive circles more inclusive. We call it building a community, and it is ultimately the most important guideline for a "sacred" childhood. Community building is hard work. It demands that we take full responsibility for our thoughts and actions, and it stretches us to evolve.

When Karen, Nina, and I first arrived at Upland Hills Farm School, the school was one month old. We met a few of the teachers and talked about education, freedom, and the curriculum, and then we walked around. There was a feeling of newness about the place. Children were in small groups, sometimes with a teacher and often without one. The school was located on Upland Hills Farm, and most of the classes were held in a large barn with a concrete floor that had two distinct rooms. One of the rooms was used as a cafeteria for visiting school groups, and the other side belonged to the school. The partition was a long series of sliding glass windows. When large school groups were being served their spaghetti lunches, they'd look through the windows at the "free school" kids. There were even days when the visiting school groups would use the upstairs barn loft as a roller skating area, and because it wasn't large enough for an oval skating pattern the skaters would start at one end of the loft and skate to the other. To us down below, it sounded and felt like we were underneath the New York subway system.

Our daughter Nina, then six years old, enjoyed her new school, and Karen and I became involved as interested parents. The growing pains of the first year became apparent just after we arrived. The director of our new school was a university professor who was only able to be at the school for two or three days a week. His magnetic personality and love of children's literature endeared him to many of his new little charges, but his absence created a vacuum. The two male teachers he had hired both arrived with significant others, and these two women were woven into the teaching staff. The forty-six or so children ranged in age from five to fifteen. They also created a wide spectrum of learning challenges. There was a child who had Down syndrome; one who was emotionally impaired; a significant number who were severely wounded by their previous public school experiences; and there were also a number of creative and talented youngsters. There was an idea that kids should be free to do what they wanted, and this created many opportunities for the emotionally troubled child to lead others into areas of delinquency, destruction, and danger.

By the middle of October, chaos and confusion had engulfed the entire community. We held meetings and began the difficult work of community building.

When I look back at our beginnings, I am reminded of how difficult birth is. Experienced from the point of view of the fetus, there's this perfect "hot springs," where all needs are met and the two are really one. For over thirty-four weeks this safe and all-encompassing environment is all the new being knows. Then at an unpredictable moment violent shaking and convulsive pressures begin. The water rushes out, and the journey to move out of the known and into the unknown begins.

The lessons of community building that we have harvested over the years begin with these growing pains. From this pain and from the chaos we moved to a stage of letting go. During this time we had to let go of our individual ideas and of our assumptions, which led to letting go of our director and two staff members. During this phase we needed to do a lot of self-examination, and we had to begin to determine if it was all worth it. Perhaps most importantly, we had to take full responsibility for all of the children who showed up on that first day of school.

Community building part two began during the summer of our second year when we actually built a geodesic dome, a well, and a septic field on a piece of land nearly half a mile from the barn we used in year one. This phase—we can call it the construction phase—is in some ways the easiest stage of community building, because we are forming the external structure and we are buoyed by daily results and our ability to solve problems. Meanwhile, we put together a team of staff members who were committed to each other and to the children. This invisible bond and group aspiration provided the engine that would make the school thrive. The board of directors got into alignment; the parent group dug in and helped fund and build the school; and by the end of year two we had become a viable entity.

The community circles you build as a parent for your children will provide the kind of nourishment and support that nothing else can. If you have an intention to create a sacred childhood for your child, you need to look for others who share similar values and yet hold different opinions. You need to be prepared to do a lot of self-examination and to let go of your fixed mind. You need to feel that the people whom you're interacting with can see the best part of who you are. True community building requires us to embrace a multicultural, inclusive mentality as if it were preparing us to live as one human family. It is an experiment in becoming a new type of human.

In the next chapter, we will see what happens when children who have a sacred childhood are released into the "wild" to express this new type of human.

Chapter Seven

WILD SALMON & WILD SCHOOLS

*The world we live in is an honorable world. To refuse this
deepest instinct of our being, to deny honor where honor
is due, to withdraw reverence from divine manifestation,
is to place ourselves on a head-on collision course with
the ultimate forces of the Universe. This question of honor
must be dealt with before any other question. We miss
both the intrinsic nature and the order of magnitude of
the issue if we place our response to the present crises
of our planet on any other basis. It is not ultimately a
political or economic or scientific or psychological issue.
It is ultimately a question of honor. Only the sense of the
violated honor of the Earth, and the need to restore this
honor, will awaken in the human the energies needed to
renew the planet in any effective manner.*

—Thomas Berry

The future is more beautiful than all the pasts.

—Pierre Teilhard de Chardin

When Thomas Berry visited our school and Ecological Awareness Center, he spoke about the pathos of the wolf and how we hunted this noble animal down to extinction. He called us the autistic generation because we are not able to hear the mountains or the rivers, the birds or the animals. He called what is happening in our times a change in the chemistry of our planet. He spoke about how it took billions of years to create the Earth's atmosphere, and in just a few decades we had already damaged it beyond repair. He urged us to develop an integral relationship between humans and the natural world and told us (Detroiters) that the automobile industry was on his short list of things that threatened the integrity of our planet.

That was in 1984, before we had heard the words "climate change and global warming." He urged us to teach our children a new story of the Universe and to begin that story 13.8 billion years ago. He spoke with the burning urgency of a man who knew that his time was running out. He was trying to wake us up so that we could hear the song and the poetry of every river and every place. He wanted us to restore honor to our planet and by doing so protect, nourish, and defend what remained.

What I learned after Thomas visited us was that he was the president of the American Teilhard Association. Pierre Teilhard de Chardin, priest, geologist, paleontologist, and futurist died in 1955. I was six years old at the time of his death, yet I would be deeply affected by his evolutionary spirit through two people who knew him intimately. His insatiable curiosity and passion for the natural world and for the cosmos were sources of inspiration that encouraged a school that was embedded in nature. It was through Thomas Berry and Jean Houston that I discovered this man who intertwined science and divinity through his writing and his life's work. When I read his words, I experienced such a deep resonance that I was inspired to learn more about biology. Paradoxically it was through these two Catholic mystics—de Chardin and Berry—that I came to appreciate the deep time of evolution, and I was encouraged to learn more about how to restore the wild. How do we restore a river? What effect would a wolf pack have if it were reintroduced into Yellowstone National Park? Is there a connection between river restoration and educating children?

When Thomas said, "There is no way of guiding the course of human affairs through the perilous course of the future except by discovering our role in this larger evolutionary process," I brought it to the attention of our staff, and we began to invent ways to experience our role as teachers that were embedded in evolution and the desire to restore the natural systems we have abused. While our school had always had nature as a prime teacher, this newly focused mission made our "wild school" not just about the future of children, but the future of all living systems.

Restoring a river is no easy task, but what we've recently learned is truly remarkable. In the Pacific Northwest, river-restoration science has led to a surprising yet inspiring conclusion. When we study one species, in this case wild salmon, and focus on all of the aspects that would enable the species to spawn, migrate, and return, the overall health of the river changes dramatically. Biologists who are currently studying the Elwha River say that the return of the salmon will benefit more than 130 species of plants and animals that have been deprived of vital food and nutrient sources for nearly a century. Everything from black bears to tiny insects and even orca whales will benefit. The salmon even fertilize the cedar trees along the river. By honoring the river the entire watershed will be restored.

Honoring the earth and our intertwined relationship to the natural world was and still is foundational to our school. That is why "sky time" has been such an important guideline for us and why our afternoon program includes numerous classes that are held "under the sky." Classes like Swamping, Trail Blazing, All-School Games, Winter Fun, Gardening, Community Supported Agriculture, Habitat Restoration, and many others have placed us in direct contact with nature. The immediacy of the natural environment as the context for our "wild school" transformed our school and sense of self. It has turned schooling "inside out" as we value the time spent outside as much as or more than time spent indoors. Thus, biology becomes more than a subject we learn about; we use all of our senses to explore, inquire, and experience biology within its true context, not just as concepts and printed words. Because of our total immersion in the natural world, we fell in love. We have been in love with nature, and in many ways she has been leading us.

In the early days of the school, I picked up a book entitled *Stalking the Wild Asparagus* by Euell Gibbons. Fueled by my own curiosity, I taught the first Wild Foods class in the spring of our school's second year, 1973. Using the book as my guide, I would take children ranging in age from five to fourteen on a hike looking for things we could eat. Each time we discovered something, we were ignited with wonder, and we began to see the world around us with new eyes. We found wild mustard, day lilies, dandelions, lambs quarters, bracken fern, cattails, and wild gobo. We prepared some of the foods during the second part of our class, and we discovered how powerful it was to be nourished by wild food.

We were like the river-restoration biologists who began their river restoration by experimenting with the idea that unimpeded river flow would be essential to the salmon's journey. We too were flowing with ideas that placed us in direct contact with the natural world, and stalking the wild asparagus was one of them. During the summer of 1972 we had to build the infrastructure of our experimental school. Assuming the role of director meant that I would also be the building contractor.

Using only the ignorance of youthful idealism and untested determination, I pulled permits, found a septic-field engineer, a well driller, and two used portable classrooms. We also began building a geodesic-dome classroom when we discovered that the two portables would allow us to be "permitted" by the state department of education, and a dome classroom could be considered a non-essential workshop.

We researched dome kits and settled on a company out West that built prefabricated hubs that could be used in conjunction with standard two-by-four's found at any local lumber yard. I ordered the hubs, sent a check, and waited. The owner of the company had assured me that the hubs would arrive in two weeks' time. They didn't. When I called to find out why, he told me that the check was not certified, and he would delay sending the hubs until he received a certified check. After asking him why he hadn't told me this to begin with and hearing him demand that it was his company and he could do anything he wanted, I hung up and lost it. It was already May, and we were waiting for the drawings before beginning any building. I flung open the screen door so forcefully I ripped it off its hinges and kicked the front step of our porch before stumbling into a ditch by the side of our old farmhouse.

My foot was throbbing with pain; my head was spinning with angst; and as I was about to let out a scream . . . I noticed a stalk of wild asparagus in front of me. I got to my feet and began following the ditch, collecting one wild asparagus after another. My mood changed without me noticing. I really didn't like asparagus at that time and had only eaten some sad, over-cooked distant relative that tasted disgusting. I took a bite of the first wild asparagus I had found, and my taste buds lit up. What was this taste? It was the taste of true essence, something I had never experienced. That taste sent me on a journey to search high and low for food in the wild. It eventually led me to the magnificent morel and the mystical maitake mushrooms. It led me to the maple trees in our forest that would yield the most magnificent sap of early spring. It rewired me to keep my eyes scanning the forest floor in search of the next treasure. I had left home a raging mess and came back transformed. A river of ideas began to flow, and soon I was in action around an entire dome kit made nearby in Davison, Michigan. A "wild idea" inspired by wild food helped us build our first building for our wild school.

For more than four decades our Wild Foods class has continued, at one point passed down to a former student who taught it for five years with renewed vitality and an expanded menu of foods. It was shortly after reading a brilliant book of essays by the poet Gary Snyder entitled The Practice of the Wild that I began to refer to our school as "a wild school." I looked up the meaning of *wild* and found "a natural state," "unpredictable," "fantastic," "any card in poker that you select," "free from conventions." That's when I realized that only the word *wild* was strong enough to liberate the word *school* from its captivity indoors and in rows and columns. I thought back to the public schools I had attended, how I hungered to be anywhere else but trapped in those stuffy rooms, a prisoner to a seat and the tyranny of the clock.

A wild school would be a place that celebrated freedom and encouraged and nurtured all relationships between humans and nature. A wild school would also be a place where imagination and creativity are honored and supported. A wild school would always be greater than the sum of its parts. Whole systems would be studied from micro systems to macro systems, and we would come to appreciate the ways systems are embedded or nested in other systems. We would allow ourselves to be led by the natural world as we fell deeper and deeper in love with her diversity, rhythms, moods, and complexities. We would try to love her as much as she loved us. We would take a vow to honor her for the rest of our lives and pass on this honoring to the generation that followed.

The key to restoring a river is to demolish all of the dams and manmade structures that have impeded its flow. The key to structuring a wild school is to demolish all of the imposed impediments to a child's sense of self-worth and curiosity. When we placed our attention on the "flow" of a school day, we discovered that these sets of activities created an environment that nourished a sense of self that was not a "thing" but more a process. For a day to flow we needed to align with it rather than manage a human-driven agenda.

The morning became a time of focus and connectedness through working in our morning-meeting groups, where teachers created comprehensive units derived from their own passions and interests, attuned to their group's developmental abilities. The line of mathematics and logic followed our morning-meeting time, but for this program groups were arranged by level, not age. Underneath this structure was an intuitive and deeply held value that there would be several breaks for children to go outside to play and come back to have something healthy to eat and drink before lunch. When we discovered how refreshing and wild filtered maple sap tasted, we encouraged our kids to take a taste directly from the spile, and a few times we brought back maple sap, filtered it, and drank it before boiling. In the fall we gathered wild apples from the old orchard throughout our campus and made wild apple cider. These tastes changed us all. There was nothing in the commercial world that tasted like wild apple cider or pure maple sap. With one drink everything changed. We had tasted the wild, and we would never be the same.

Rivers meander; they do not flow in straight lines. Wild schools also meander. We structure our days and our trimesters in ways that allow for spontaneity and investigation. When an ice storm knocks out our main power lines, we have the ability to operate the school by using a number of integrated alternative systems. From 1973 to this very moment there are systems in place to produce electricity, pump water, and heat the school. The days that we have decided not to close but to operate using these systems are dynamic opportunities for our children to have direct experiences with living off the grid. The curriculum varies to include these ways of operating so that our children pay attention to things like toilet flushing, light, heat, and communication.

Another key to river restoration is "natural variability." All ecosystems have natural variability, but rivers in particular vary by their rate of flow. To restore a river, this natural variability needs to be reestablished if possible, and when it is, everything changes. The river begins to flow in ways that create a wide range of habitat types and ecosystem processes that maintain the natural biological diversity of aquatic and streamside species. A major consequence of this natural variability is that all species experience favorable conditions at some time, preventing any one species from dominating.

In a wild school natural variability is connected to the seasonal flow and rhythms of the natural world. In the fall we come back to begin a school year after "ripening" during the summer. The waning days of summer are such a great time to begin a journey. The first days of our coming together have been designed to welcome, celebrate, orient, and taste our way into the adventure that is about to unfold. There is a welcoming ceremony for the new children where our oldest kids give a rose to the new ones. There are three field trips that literally take the whole school into or across the farm fields to the farm, then over the old orchard to a field where the Ecological Awareness Center is, and finally to the field where our community garden is. Each place holds some big magic for each group of children.

Upland Hills Farm has been in operation since 1960 and is dedicated to teaching children where our food and fiber come from. The flow for the children at the farm is exuberant play on huge hay stacks; a farm show that includes milking a cow and making butter; play on the innovative play grounds that include large boulders; old tractors and climbing structures; and fresh bread for the butter the children made. The flow at our Upland Hills Ecological Awareness Center includes a tour of the living roof; a dance with the solar panels that follow the sun; eating something that was cooked in our solar oven; a group-by-group exploration of UV light; the pedal-powered scavenger hunt; and a demonstration of how to design with nature.

On the Friday of our first week back, we celebrate the opening week by making wild apple cider, solar bruschetta, roasted sweet corn, and playing all-school games—a version of capture the flag played on a large field with the oldest group challenging the entire rest of the school. By the end of the short three-day week, each student in the oldest group has designed and made their own chair that they will use for the two years they are in that group, and our year is off and running.

The winter flow is tied directly to the weather. The flow is slower, and we adjust to daily changes by making art, rehearsing plays, doing music, and experiencing winter fun. We go inward as a school, and it culminates in our arts-and-science festival held in late February. The maple trees' first run is our clue that spring is about to emerge, but we know how many weather shifts are possible in Michigan in any given year, and we flow with the weather, never fully embracing spring until the last days of April or even the occasional May snow or ice event.

Our river is rushing by the end of April and the beginning of May, and it moves with a force, power, and determination that doesn't let up until the last three days of school. The last three days of school begin with an all-school presentation where each of the graduates presents their senior project. This passion-based project was selected by the senior, presented before the entire staff, and then explained in front of the entire school. We've been doing senior projects for nearly two decades now, and they never disappoint. They range from Kate's tile mosaic that greets everyone who enters the Karen Joy Theatre to Jackie's hand-made book of poetry and drawings depicting her story at Upland Hills from her first day of school until her last.

The afternoon of that same day we present the awards to the children who have earned the status of Renaissance person, celebrating their broad range of study. Starting with the third youngest group (ages seven through eight), each child can choose their afternoon classes so they participate in all seven areas of study offered, including the performing arts, natural science, applied science, community service, language arts, the visual arts, and independent study. We have created a complex set of distinctions designed to give incentives for children to become comprehensivists who can also discover and focus on a passion that resonates deeply with their own soul.

The last two days of each school year include an all-school overnight that begins with a talent show on Thursday afternoon. The flow of this extended time together moves from setting up tents to dinner, a model-rocket launch, an all-school birthday dance around the campfire, and a series of songs for the youngest to the oldest groups. Each group is dismissed by a song until only the oldest group is left. They hold the space for us all as day shifts into night. This time belongs to them as they sing their favorite songs, share some stories, and discover the magic of the night underneath the tree canopy in the valley between the school and the Ecological Awareness Center.

The morning on the last day of school begins with home-made French toast. The day holds a space for a student film festival, playing, socializing, and preparing the theatre for the graduation ceremony. Leaving a little more than an hour, we call the entire school into the theatre for the graduation ceremony.

Parents, friends, and family members gather to acknowledge the five to ten eighth graders who will be moving on to a new school or to home schooling. Each student will be called to the stage, and their educational journey will be told as they sit on the elevated stool to receive insightful, humorous, and tender words from the audience. The person being acknowledged takes over as they call on people who would like to share. They hear from the youngest kids—"You are the nicest person I know"—to their current and former classmates—"You made me feel like I finally belonged." The flow of these sacred last moments of the school year is filled with creative, unscripted comments that arise out of our community spontaneously. These words are given and received as the gifts of our deep inter-relatedness and their time being a part of our wild school.

For more than three decades, we have ended the school year with a song written by John Lennon and Paul McCartney, "The Long and Winding Road." It feels like it was written for us, as we live on Indian Lake Road, which is a winding dirt road, but it was written about a road in Scotland that travels to Oban, where Paul and Linda raised their children. It was the very same road that Karen, Nina, and I lived on when we lived in Scotland for a month, exactly one year before we discovered Upland Hills School.

There must be great excitement when the river scientists and naturalists release the native salmon into a restored river in the hopes that they will spawn, migrate, and return. We too are very excited about releasing our kids into the complex world we live in at this crucial time of our evolutionary development. We have been sending our children into the world since 1972, and we have gathered some evidence of how their "wild school" education has played a significant role in their decisions and actions.

The life cycle of human beings forces us to confront how unpredictable any one life is from birth until death. In my role as the director of an independent school it felt as if every child were in some inexplicable way mine. In trying to convey this feeling, words fall far short of the experience. I didn't think of them in the same way as I did Nina and Sasha, but there was and continues to be this distinct, unbreakable connection. I felt responsible for their safety, for their happiness, and for preparing them to live a balanced life in a world out of balance. I carried them with me in my consciousness as if there were no separation between us. When we planted a peace pole for our twenty-fifth anniversary, we made a name plaque for each child who had died. When I sat next to it, I'd look at those names and contemplate the events of that child's life and marvel at the mystery of who they were, when they lived, what they left us, and how they died. These were some of the wild children who came through us to help us to awaken and to grow.

Every one of them left our lives changed. It is not their names we remember; it is the gifts they gave to each of us and to this place that live on.

Bruce was a child who would often follow me around, talking about things that interested him. I experienced him as a stream of words and ideas and quickly noticed how the other children often tired of his incessant monologue. He was clearly a child who often found himself on the margins of our community. I too found it challenging to be with him sometimes, although other times I found him funny and insightful. I often invited him to give me a hand with some menial task like shoveling dirt into a wheelbarrow or stacking fire wood, and he would usually ignore the request and keep on talking.

On the next to last day of his life he showed up at school with a tricked out VW Bug that he had made into a dune buggy. He was in his late teens and had often talked about doing something with a VW car frame, and now here he was ready to give his old teacher the ride of his life. I asked him to help me finish what I was doing before we went on the ride, and to my amazement he actually pitched in as we dug into the earth to plant asparagus roots for future use.

With more than a little trepidation I sat in the passenger seat, strapped myself in as firmly as possible, and off we went. I marveled at the role reversal aspect, with him in the driver's seat and me along for the ride. He talked about all of the engineering he had done by himself as we climbed hills and splashed through a few wet areas. I was impressed and ready to be done when he took a sharp turn and climbed straight up Grasshopper Hill. With my heart in my throat I looked up at the sky praying that we wouldn't flip. When we came to a stop, he was convulsing in fits of laughter. I must have been ghost white as I gladly unbuckled and stood on terra firma.

I walked him to the parking lot, and as he drove his dune buggy onto the trailer I told him that he really impressed me.

"Why?" he asked.

"Because I didn't know if you'd actually do it."

"Oh, I was just in my design phase," he answered.

As he drove out of the parking lot, I watched him disappear down the road. The next time I'd see him he would be in a coffin having died of a brain aneurism. The peace pole that was planted twenty years after that day was planted at the top of Grasshopper Hill. The shock of the news of his death will never leave me. I couldn't have imagined a more alive Bruce than the one who showed up that day. He had shown the one who had listened that he could make something, and his last day on earth was dedicated to a thrill ride that would last a lifetime.

The Power of the Wind

Jesse grew up loving the natural world. It was a primary relationship that began before he could remember. The oldest of three boys, his parents raised him to run freely over the seventeen acres that surrounded the house that they built. By the time they enrolled him in our school he was already bound by this relationship to nature to be outside as much as possible. For the seven years that he was a part of our school community he loved the freedom that encouraged him to put his hands in the earth and his bare feet on the ground. In Wild Foods class he learned how to identify, gather, and prepare wild mushrooms, something he enjoys to this day. He reported one year on the number of morels he had found, and when I asked where he found them he simply smiled and said, "Where the mycelium was just right." He also loved using tools and building things. At the precocious age of seven he was working side by side with his father, a high school math teacher who ran a deck-building company on the side.

Jesse learned how to collaborate with others through the theatre and through the many group projects that grew in complexity each year. He spent many hours in our wind-powered dome workshop using special DC-powered tools to drill, saw, and sand the things he made. He was curious about the way things worked and had an uncommon, persistent nature that could not be defeated. He was as fascinated as I was when the wind-generator meter would deflect forward indicating that between 2 to 8 amps were flowing directly into our battery bank, storing power for future use.

He formed strong friendship bonds with many of his class-mates that somehow had this mix of serious intent seasoned with wild mischief. When he was finishing what would be his seventh-grade year, he decided that it was time for him to move on from Upland Hills School. He came up to me one day and told me that some of his closest friends were in eighth grade, and that, coupled with the fact that he had gotten everything he needed from us, was the reason he wanted to leave. I had come to know him well enough by this time to appreciate his forthright, transparent nature and to know this was already a decision he had made, not an opportunity for a conversation. The die had already been cast.

We kept in touch during his high school years, because his two younger brothers were still attending Upland Hills and I had formed a close relationship with both of his parents. I heard about his very last day of high school from his mom. He and a friend were drinking beer in his parents' car while parked in their driveway just a few feet from the road. A po-liceman turned on his lights and sounded his siren, prompting Jesse's friend to throw the remains of the six-pack out of the car window as Jesse drove down the driveway. They were ticketed, resulting in a large fine, and they were both given probation for six months. When I heard about it, I thought about the ab-surdity of the entire event. First, being arrested in your own driveway, in a parked car, drinking beer, which while techni-cally illegal was not a big deal to his very conscious and caring parents; the panic of his friend, who threw the evidence right into the possession of the police; and the (drunk?) drive of a thousand feet to the barn. It all seemed like slapstick comedy to me. It wasn't the least bit funny to Jesse or to his parents.

His next brush with the law came two years later. It too in-volved cars and alcohol, but this time an unintended rite of passage was thrown in. He had attended a university for a short time, always asking the questions, What do I want to do? and Am I wasting money and time here? When he returned home, he enrolled in the local community college without purpose or intention.

This time when the police lights and siren were approaching he and his two friends abandoned his parents' car while it was still rolling and fled. It was winter, bone-chilling winter, in the wee hours of the morning and Jesse running full tilt fell down. He got up, bleeding and injured, and kept running. A policeman flashed his light right in Jesse's direction, threatened to shoot, and once again, Jesse ran. Injured, scared, alone, and bleeding he managed to walk the twelve miles overland to his home by using the moonlight and his excellent sense of direction. He arrived home to his frightened parents, who thought he was dead, along with two policemen and the car.

This time, the police took pity on his parents and this feckless lad. The rural county dropped all charges and slapped him with a $100 fine. However, when the court discovered his two probation violations from the first offense, he was summoned to appear before a judge.

When the judge called Jesse, he stood without an attorney, and with his voice shaking from fear, he told her the entire truth from start to unblemished finish. His lucid, heartfelt confession moved the judge to set him aside until the end of the day. In her chambers she confided that she had been prepared to give him thirty days in jail, no questions asked. She then told him that when he acknowledged that as an adult "You are responsible for everything you do, and you must own it," she changed her mind. She instructed him to perform community service and offered to have lunch sometime.

I hired Jesse and his friend to help build the Karen Joy Theatre in the summer of 2003. Jesse and I would meet every morning and go over the steps it would take to finish the theatre. I watched from the front row as he took on each job with drive, determination, and problem-solving skills far beyond his years. We worked well together because I had always seen his potential, and he knew how much I trusted him. I was much more of a coach than a contractor. Over just a few months, I watched as he rebuilt himself. He and his friend applied the outside and inside concrete finish; they installed the seats; they hung the ceiling; and they built the sound booth. As each step was completed his confidence grew as well. On his last day of work we stood together in awe and gratitude. With tears in my eyes I thanked him for making a dream a reality. He smiled and said, "We couldn't let Karen down."

He enrolled in a university located in the Upper Peninsula of Michigan after deciding that he wanted to earn a degree in construction management. On his drive over the Mackinac Bridge he saw two 900 kilowatt wind turbines and wondered about their construction. They looked like beautiful giants, titans of a new age.

He earned his degree and got an interview with the vice president and human resources manager of a large wind energy company located in Minnesota, who offered him a position. When asked about his interest in wind power, he replied quite truthfully, "I've known about the power of the wind since I was six years old."

During his years working for that company, he discovered three important things about himself and the industry he loves. The first one was that he hated working in the office and much preferred to be on-site supervising the entire installation process, from site preparation to the moment when the 1.6 megawatt generator produces its first surge of electrical energy. The second thing he learned was that he hungered to call his own shots, to form his own company. The third thing he learned was that the 120 bolts—each 20 feet long—that fastened these huge machines to earth were in danger of rusting and loosening over time.

The company he founded, Windsecure, has a patent to prevent these systems from crashing to the ground. His company inspects the foundations of these megawatt wind systems, and Jesse, along with his team (which includes his father), manages, supervises, inspects, and invents the tools to make sure that these beautiful giants are safe and secure. He told me recently that this quote from Muhammad Ali has helped him get to where he is today: "It's repetition of affirmations that leads to belief, and once that belief becomes a deep conviction, things begin to happen."

With the birth of his son and most recently his daughter, Jesse's life is full. Things are happening on a large scale for his small company. He is doing what he loves in the industry that he believes in with all of his heart. His family is in the center of every decision and every moment of his life. He knows that producing electrical power from a non-polluting, renewable source of energy is a gift for the generations that will follow, but for Jesse it is as simple as knowing that his son and daughter deserve to grow up in a world that is powered by the sun and the wind. This is sustainable; this is honorable; this is the paradigm shift that will take us into the future.

It will take a generation for the Elwha River to be fully restored, but already we have learned much from this marvelous initiative. The near-shore environment where the river meets the sea is changing by leaps and bounds. It appears that the renewed sediment flow has created an environment that is perfectly suited for shellfish beds, which are already reemerging. Releasing wild children into the "river" of these challenging yet promising times is also having an effect.

Jesse's story is about someone who had the courage to form a new company that was an expression of his passion for building and his deep love for the natural world. The hundreds of children who were given the opportunity to flow in a stream that was more wild than tame will have effects as unpredictable as the benefits of river restoration.

As for Tom Berry's lamenting of the loss of the wolf, he'd be so pleased to know about the trophic cascade that is underway in Yellowstone National Park. In 1995 the grey wolf was reintroduced into the park. That single effort has astonished scientists and biologists all over the globe. The effect of the wolf has cascaded like a waterfall throughout the entire park ecosystem. The elk and the deer are stronger; the aspens and willows are healthier; and the beaver colonies have gone from one to nine in just two decades. The rivers are running deeper and faster as the entire scientific community rethinks the role of top predatory species.

Wild salmon and wild schools are linked by their love of the natural world. If today's adults come to recognize and embrace the power of this relationship between children and nature, a new creative energy will be released. Schools could become the engines of innovation if only they have the courage and willingness to blow up the dams and let the rivers flow.

What if wild schools became evolutionary laboratories? What if we answered the age-old question, "Why do I have to learn that?" by answering it with, "Because you are integral to the evolutionary path that began fourteen billion years ago." What if we invited our children to stand on the edge of evolution, invited them to link arms, and empowered them to repair, heal, invent, create, and build a world that worked in harmony with the cosmos?

The future of children, and perhaps human life on earth, stands on evolution's edge.

Chapter Eight

EVOLUTION'S EDGE

It's amazing to realize that every species on the planet right now is going to be shaped primarily by its interaction with humans. It was never that way before. For three billion years, life evolved in a certain way; all of this evolution took place in the wilds. But now, it is the decisions of humans that are going to determine the way this planet functions and looks for hundreds of millions of years in the future. Our power has gotten ahead of us, has gotten ahead of our consciousness. This is a challenge we've never faced before: to relearn to be human in a way that is actually enhancing to these other creatures.

—Brian Swimme, cosmologist

To relearn to be human in a way that supports and nourishes all of life on this planet is the challenge of this time. When I first heard Brian Swimme say that the relationship between the Earth and the Sun was a love story, I felt it. Evolution itself became a story of how the unfolding of everything that occurred from the very beginning of the great flaring forth to the moment when the first cells were formed was transformed from scientific information into a sacred story. The ninety-three million miles between the Earth and Sun; the size of the earth after a meteor tore off what is now our moon; the oval orbits of the planets; the shape and the size of the Milky Way; it all was leading to life and eventually to us. Evolution led to the development of a species that was designed to be forever young, the one mammalian species that prolongs childhood. Evolution, a continual process of incompleteness, led directly to a species that was specialized in only one thing, and that one thing is the ability to learn. It has taken us these last ten thousand years to get to this point where a deep inner subjective knowing, a new kind of self-reflection, can catch up with our ability to create and destroy. Now, because of the imminent dangers we have created here on earth and because we are connected to each other as never before, we can take the next evolutionary step to a future that is more conscious and more connected.

The idea of a love-based education grew out of this cosmic love story or, as Tom Berry and Brian Swimme called it, "the universe story." Love and evolution go hand in hand. The ultimate creative expression is the ever-expanding and continually changing universe. When we consider that we are now evolution's edge, we must activate a collective love that can create a synergy beyond anything that we have ever experienced. We got sidetracked along the way by attending schools that practiced divide and conquer so that now we are conditioned to behave like conquistadors instead of sustainers. These industrial schools were so deeply rooted in the idea that children were things to be processed and that schooling was supposed to be painful, boring, mind numbing, and difficult that it has taken us far too long to break out of these prisons of the spirit. Love is the driving force behind the universe story. From the birth of stars to the birth of a child, our universe is counting on love.

What if there were millions of schools that were all deeply aligned with the same context? What if that context were based on our cumulative knowledge of evolution? What if these evolutionary schools taught us about meaning, purpose, play, creativity, and passion? What if these schools aspired to teach our children how to live in a loving way, based on loving our planet and each other? What if we took our place in the evolutionary process that began fourteen billion years ago and became responsible co-creators of the evolutionary process? We have all heard the phrase "children are our future," but what if we took that simple saying as a directive? That at this moment in the fourteen-billion-year-old evolutionary story humanity must awaken to the idea that we are deeply connected to that long-ago moment when our universe flared forth. Our reason to be is to join in that process and to act as if every action, every word, every decision has a huge ramification as to the continued health of our planet. We must transform into a species of protectors.

In the book *Evolutionaries*, Carter Phipps writes,

Evolution is a fact... I would say that I believe in evolution, only I don't think belief has anything to do with it. We don't say we believe the world is round—we know it is... The idea of evolution, the basic notion of process, change, and development over time, is affecting much more than biology. It is affecting everything, from our perceptions of politics, economics, psychology, and ecology to our understanding of the most basic constituents of reality... Evolution ... is certainly about the birds and bees, but it's also about culture, consciousness, and the cosmos... Taken as a whole, it will constitute the organizing principle of a new worldview, uniquely suited for the twenty-first century and beyond.

The evangelicals of today that believe the biblical version of how things came to be are much like our deep-time ancestors who were hunters and gatherers. Fear of breaking a pattern, and fear of the unknown combine to keep us comfortable with what is. So many of us were frightened by the future and set on living in the status quo. For close to four million years we wandered in small bands without possessions, living as wild animals with big brains. Because we live on a spherical planet we eventually ran into each other, having populated much of our earth. But then something happened about ten thousand years ago that changed everything. We became domesticated. We settled beside four major rivers and began a journey that created abundance, laws, domination, war, slavery, and something we now call civilization. We probably didn't want to make this change; we were afraid to leave the world of wandering, because it was an ingrained pattern; but the allure of abundant food and security must have been stronger than the life of a nomad.

This fear of massive change causes us to cling to what we know and what we have become habituated to, but our curiosity draws us forward. As Teilhard says, we grope along as we progress.

In our school we were given the opportunity to build bridges between people who believed in creation theory and those of us who were determined to teach from the largest context we could imagine, which eventually became the universe story. One of our teachers, who had graduated from Wayne State University's college of humanistic psychology, underwent a transformation of faith during his years with us. He and his wife, who met during their years at the college of humanistic psychology, were deeply touched and influenced by another of our staff members who believed and lived a life that was embedded in her love and devotion to her absolute faith in the life and teachings of Jesus Christ. This relationship eventually led to their conversion from a secular humanistic point of view to a Christ-centered worldview. Our working relationship throughout this conversion continued to be strong because of the bonds of our friendships, but these bonds would be tested throughout the years.

During a teacher-parent conference, a parent confronted this newly converted teacher with his use of the New Testament in his classroom. I became aware of it and engaged him in a conversation about the inappropriate use of the Bible within our school curriculum. I also invited his mentor/teacher in on the conversation. We sat for over an hour discussing the situation and left with the understanding that as a teacher at Upland Hills School direct quotes as injunctions from the Old or New Testament would not be shared in any of our classrooms.

When he talked about it with his mentor, she emphasized the point that his over-zealousness was in fact an indication that his faith was still fragile and that he needed to live his faith instead of preaching it. She went on to say that the beauty of our school was that we were encouraged to teach about all faiths and that we also welcomed parents who were agnostics and atheists. We used our love of childhood, our love of the wild, and our love of each other to animate a curriculum that was filled with spirit. This, she said, was the key to our being able to work with children in a new way. She had already experienced many years of being able to find that openness and truth in her students, and this enabled her to do depth work beyond anything she dreamed possible. The newly converted—and newly "schooled"—teacher listened and took it deeply into his heart.

We all found a place that lived beyond our opinions, values, and beliefs. It was through our relationships, our trust in each other, and our ability to get beyond the dogma of belief that we were able to navigate this new territory of working in a school that was a blend of our better selves. Our mutual love was forged in our hearts and tested by the tensions of self-righteousness. This self-righteousness occurred on all sides and was mediated by our love for the children and our bond of friendship with each other.

My role as a teacher is to prepare children for the world in such a way as to empower them to eventually take over. I have learned over time that learning how to learn is the essential foundation for everything we know. I have come to realize that everything we do and think is connected to others. We stand on the shoulders of the first story tellers, mathematicians, scientists, engineers, musicians, artists, and writers, and we continue to benefit from their contemporaries. My experience thus far has led me to a worldview that was shaped by my teachers and tested by my experiences. Being born into a loving family and being someone who was born into a world of abundance and plenitude, I developed my ability to trust, to risk, and to love. I knew at an early age that by the standards of my grades and my test results I was regarded as "an average" student, with little creative potential. I knew that I was in the middle of somewhere, yet I also knew that the game, the way I was being judged and evaluated, was unjust. With just that little kernel of awareness I followed a path that led me to question the way things were and to journey beyond the boundaries of convention.

I know, in my limited way, that our earth is in peril. I also know that the mechanical systems we have developed and derived to educate children are mostly irrelevant to the crucial issues of our time, whether it be climate change or global conflict. I believe that every child's education should connect to our species' evolutionary purpose, which is to collaborate at the highest levels in order to reverse, remediate, and restore the life-support systems onboard Spaceship Earth.

What would our schools look like if they were dedicated to practicing evolution? How would the curriculum of early childhood education differ from our current model? What key foundational differences would drive schools that taught four to fourteen year olds? How would we transform high schools into places that engaged students so totally that these teenagers would become a force for creative change? How would higher education change to meet the needs of a world that depended on it to produce the most creative, collaborative, inventive, inclusive, and innovative leaders that our globe has ever seen?

Thomas Berry and Brian Swimme used the term *Ecozoic Era* to describe a possible future where humans can live in a mutually enhancing relationship with our planet and the earth community. Which is why Brian Swimme thinks that the fastest way for us to wake up is to realize that at this very moment our planet is in the midst of a mass extinction of our own making. The Ecozoic Era depends on a collective awakening on the part of humanity that is led by our youth. It can only occur if more adults and teachers also wake up and become more conscious so that we can create together new environments and conditions that will encourage creative, collective actions on behalf of all of life. This is why I call this chapter "Evolution's Edge." We are currently living on this edge, and we have come to a time when everything depends on us. If we are to save what's left of all the remaining species on this planet, then we need to think, relate, and act in new ways that are in alignment with a new era, an Ecozoic Era.

Evolution and the Universe Story teaches us some very powerful lessons that we can immediately offer and apply to our children:

1. Forever young: schools that encourage children to play are places that are serving the cosmos.

2. Schools that develop, encourage, and support deep inter-subjective exploration are schools that know the importance of sacred communion.

3. Schools that are different and that honor individual differences are places where evolution can advance our species.

4. Schools that strive to be places of unity are schools that prepare us for a world that works for all.

When we applied these four lessons at our school, we experienced love. Our school is small, and it seems that perhaps one of the biggest changes that education needs to embrace is the idea that small is beautiful. The industrial era produced schools that looked, felt, and even smelled like factories. This may have seemed very efficient at the time, but now more than ever we need to feel safe, known, trusted, loved, understood, and valued. This can only happen in small groups.

Our ancestors who developed around 200,000 years ago emerged from Africa, and within a fraction of a cosmic second we found ourselves everywhere. We now know that our ancestors, being led by burning curiosity and wild game, left Africa and in just 150,000 years were dispersed all over the earth. From the deserts of Australia to the jungles of South America our upright, hands-free, big-brained, tool-making predecessors, as hunter gatherers, were roaming in bands of between twenty-five and forty people. This was our first group size until the early civilizations developed, just 10,000 years ago.

When our school began, it was also that size. There were many reasons for this, from the outside-the-box premise of the school to the need to sustain it financially. But this small size made it possible for us to be nimble and responsive, viable when we contracted, and accommodating when we grew.

A Curriculum Designed for Evolution's Edge

Evolution and learning how to learn go hand in hand. Schools that are guided by the Universe Story, so beautifully told in books and film by Brian Swimme and Thomas Berry, are places that inspire us to grow and to know. At our school we used "Man a Course of Study," Kees Boeke's *Cosmic View: The Universe in 40 Jumps*, and Huck Scarry's book *Our Earth* to create a context large enough for children to relate to and to fall in love with. We were also blessed with Carl Sagan's master work *Cosmos*, which inspired our staff to tell parts of this story in our classrooms, in the forest, on the farm, and by the edge of a pond, swamp, or great lake.

Even though we were challenged with an overabundance of material, we knew that children could linger at any one place and find awe and wonder in the smallest details, and that's what we were after. We intentionally let go of the millions of tasks and details of traditional school subjects and instead focused on context. This enlarged context was based on the scientific discoveries of the last century. We were now teaching comprehensive units that were directly linked to evolutionary journeys. We thought of our work as guides who were there to protect the child's natural curiosity and to encourage them to always think in terms of relatedness. We used poetry, songs, stories, films, art, and experiments to capture and enchant our children.

Every day our curriculum offered one invitation after another for children to learn by doing and to learn how to learn. We taught the stars through the sun. We used the artifacts that were built in our summer workshops for the Ecological Awareness Center to make solar soup, bake bread, start fires, warm coats, heat the dome and the Ecological Awareness Center, purify water, and dry fruit. We also used the sun to tell time and to make art. We introduced children at a very early age to the speed of light and talked about the time it took for light to travel the ninety-three million miles from the sun to our earth. We used Bucky's metaphor of Spaceship Earth, and we emphasized the spin and zip of our spaceship. We even used his idea of eliminating the earth-centric idea of a sunrise or sunset and used the words sunsight and sunclipse instead.

One of our teachers who loved science taught an entire comprehensive unit every other year for fifth and sixth graders on astronomy, complete with an evening of telescopes and star gazing. We also taught model-rocket building from the very first year. We built rockets that had two stages; rockets that took movies from the apogee of the flight; rockets that turned into gliders; and rockets that carried a payload. It was easy to justify to our parent group the teaching of these classes. The hard science of Jan's comprehensive unit on astronomy was backed with great movies like *The Right Stuff* and *October Sky*, and it brought out all of the parents and grandparents who owned telescopes. With the rocket class we taught trigonometry by using a simple altitude instrument and calculating the height of the flight, usually 1,100 feet. Yet the real intention behind presenting these classes was to instill adventure, a sense of wonder, the power of teamwork, and the pure delight of the round-trip of lifting off the planet and returning home.

From an evolutionary point of view we were joining our ancient ancestors who told stories about the stars, painted them on the ceilings of small churches, and marveled at just what they were and how they moved. This ancient screen of day- and night-time sky was now being celebrated and used with our kids, and this connection, we now know, lasts for an entire lifetime.

Juno Orbits Jupiter with an Assist from Upland Hills School

When Eric invited us to a rocket launch at Cape Canaveral, we were thrilled. As the chief test conductor at Lockheed Martin, it was Eric who gave the official "Go" for the spacecraft to launch. For Karen and I, it was proof that our work could result in something far beyond our wildest imagination.

Our student Eric loved the theatre, and he loved science. Our school had also introduced him to our adventure playground, which he loved. Spending four days with him and his family in Florida allowed us to plumb the mystery of that moment when MAVEN rumbled and ignited as it lifted off the Earth to travel to Mars.

MAVEN'S mission was to conduct a series of experiments over a period of nine years to discover what happened to the water on Mars and to its atmosphere. Our mission during our four-day window of living close to each other was to connect the child we knew to the adult he had become. Both missions revealed much about the evolution of relationship and the need for a paradigm shift.

Eric talked about the launch sequence as being similar to a live performance of theatre. He told us that the work they had done as children putting on plays and performing in front of a live audience had prepared him to be the central person who was in charge of all of the electrical spacecraft-level testing. The same kid who used direct current from our battery bank that was charged by our Dunlite wind generator was in charge of every electrical aspect of this rocket. The kid who acted in *James and the Giant Peach* grew into the man whom everyone on his team trusted.

He spoke about participating with members of his MBA class on team-building exercises very similar to our ropes course. He immediately gravitated to those who were most anxious and timid around the challenges and instinctively offered coaching and support for each of them. He quickly realized that his childhood experiences on our adventure playground were benefiting not just him but his classmates as well. The paradigm shift that is required in the world of rockets and space exploration is centered on collaboration and developing a group mind. He had direct experiences of some of those skills when he was eleven years old and now was using what he learned about group problem-solving with the engineers and scientists at Lockheed.

MAVEN launched on November 18, 2013, and we celebrated the launch and Karen's birthday together in Florida as two extended, blended families. A few days after the launch we gathered our crew for a field trip. Eric and his pregnant wife and child, and his brother Andy and his wife and two children, as well as our daughter Sasha, who was filming the launch for our school, all gathered to launch model rockets. We had used some of the spare time together to build several model rockets. We went to a park on Merritt Island for lunch and a launch.

The laughter, preparation, equipment adjustments, and role assignments created an atmosphere that was a hybrid of déjà vu and who is who. We set off at least seven rockets and recovered every one. There seemed to be no distinctions between the children and the adults; we were all playing as one. In a moment of calm while Eric and Andy and their children were searching for a rocket named Big Bertha, I experienced this deep sense of joy. Eric and Andy were both adults and children to me, and I too was both; it felt as if we had been playing together for over two decades. A dream or parts of many dreams had come together in that moment. Andy and his wife were sending their children to our school, and Andy was finishing his degree as an engineer. Each of our dreams had blended into a kind of unity, and the evolutionary result was that we were actualizing and living from a new consciousness that belonged to something beyond our individualized selves. This fluency between our adult selves and our childlike joy and curiosity felt like it was an inherent design aspect of our species. Our species was designed to flow directly into play so that creative insights might arise.

In October of 2014, one month after MAVEN entered into orbit around Mars, Eric and his family visited our school. He wanted to talk about creating a charter school that he and his wife had already named Ardor. When they arrived, we toured the school and finally sat down to talk about their ideas. Inspired by the birth of their two children, they were determined to send them to a school that would embrace passion and cultivate life-long curiosity. As I listened, it was easy to find resonance with how we felt as we were inventing our school. They wanted their school to prepare their children for the future. They wanted their school to empower children to take charge of their own education, and they wanted their teachers to teach from their passion. They wanted their children to have direct experiences with the natural world and to be able to interact with each other with a skill and nimbleness that demonstrated a depth of knowledge of interpersonal intelligence.

My experience of being with them that afternoon was one of great admiration. I admired how deeply devoted they were to being conscious parents who wanted their children to thrive. I also admired their deep commitment to education and Eric's willingness to leave a job he loved to make sure his children were educated in ways that both parents valued most.

The most rewarding job Eric has had was the spacecraft named Juno. Juno launched in August of 2011. Its mission is to provide the most in-depth and comprehensive study of the composition of Jupiter to date. Juno has already set the record for the fastest manmade object ever, and it is also the first solar-powered spacecraft that has broken the record for traveling the furthest distance from the sun.

The launch date for Juno was set based on the orbits of the planets and could not be readjusted, which means the deadline must be met or you have to wait a long time before the alignment occurs again. It's like launching a rocket through a keyhole in space. His team was constantly working weekends and overtime to keep pace with the planets as they encountered one challenge after another. Eric was the lead engineer for all of the mechanical operations involving the Juno spacecraft. He soon discovered, and would state it clearly in a team meeting, that building the spacecraft was the easy part; learning how to work effectively with a large team provided both the greatest challenge and biggest reward.

Eric's team was nested inside of many other teams. Long before Lockheed Martin began building Juno, other teams throughout the world were engaged in designing experiments that might be selected to travel onboard a spacecraft that might one day orbit Jupiter.

Juno's mission is to better understand Jupiter's formation and evolution. Two of the questions our scientists are asking are, Does it have a solid core? and How does it produce its gigantic magnetic fields? Jupiter's size, two times the size of all of the planets in our solar system put together, gives us an opportunity to discover how planets form. Jupiter's size means that its formation has been dramatically slower than every other planet in our solar system.

Eric was the operations lead for Juno as it was being built. He oversaw the day-to-day operations of assembly and construction. He thought of himself as Juno's steward. It was Eric who oversaw the crane operations and the transportation aspect of putting Juno on a C-17 aircraft for delivery to Cape

Canaveral. It was also his observation that every engineering aspect went through multiple reviews; however there was little preparation for how the humans of every team would interact with each other.

Eric's own evolution occurred during Juno's birth. He wanted people to work in harmony, but he first had to learn what drives us and what motivates us. In order to do that, he had to look inward and develop his own insight. The test that was the catalyst for his inner growth occurred when he was introduced to the project director of the Jovian Infrared Auroral Mapper (JIRAM), which was built in Torino, Italy.

His first impression of JIRAM's team leader was that he was a forceful, passionate, pushy guy who wanted to test this mild-mannered young engineer that Lockheed put in charge of the magnificent Juno. Eric stood his ground as he sweated bullets. Soon the two men were in a standoff, as precious time was passing. Eric went home carrying the perfect conditions for an upset stomach and a sleepless night. It was then that he did some research and discovered that this man and his team had been working on this leading-edge image spectrometer long before Eric came to Lockheed.

As a young father, he understood how this man was going to make darn sure his team's invention was going to be placed right and taken care of. The next morning when they met Eric gave his full attention to his nemesis and disarmed him by starting with, "Tell me all you can about JIRAM and let me know what I can touch and what I can't touch."

As they circled the spectrometer, Eric listened intently and commented on the brilliance of this new generation of image spectrometers and of the possible views it might send us from deep space. The two men had come into an alignment. They discussed options and found common ground.

On August 27, 2016, Juno sent us the first images of Jupiter's north pole, and it was not at all like anything we had ever seen or imagined. We also received detailed, high-resolution images from the Jovian Infrared Auroral Mapper. JIRAM found hot spots that have never been seen before. We also heard Jupiter's auroras for the first time, thanks to Waves, an instrument that recorded the signature emissions of the energetic particles that generate the massive auroras.

Through one of our students we have been taken directly to evolution's edge. We are now able to see things that we've never seen and learn things that we never knew. We are even listening to sounds that may contain clues to the origin of our solar system. Through Eric, his family, his team members, his children, his developing collaboration skills, we are also on Juno's journey.

Our earliest ancestors, as in the first life forms, were bacteria. We have recently discovered that water and its ability to dissolve minerals was most likely the way that rocks came to life. In the ocean off the coast of Iceland we discovered a thermal vent at the end of a huge water column and speculate that this is how life began. As Juno orbits Jupiter with its eight instruments harvesting new images, sounds, and data, we curious bipeds are on the frontier of knowing where we come from and who we are. Scientists are speculating about one of Jupiter's moons, Europa. They believe that this moon has all of the factors that could produce life. Europa is a rocky place with a huge ocean of water under its frozen crust. If there is a hot spot in the interior of that moon, then the lines we see from Earth may in fact be forms of life.

The excitement that we—his teachers, his family, his friends—feel is an excitement that transcends the individual. Our species, via Eric and his colleagues, is investigating through their imaginations, skills, creativity, collaborative bonds, and full-on curiosity the origins of our solar system. One answer as to why we are who we are could be that we are this way because we are an integral part of that first creative act of the great flaring forth.

As I sat in my home and heard the sounds of an aurora while watching the images of JIRAM reveal an amazing picture of Jupiter's south pole and the auroras, I felt this unbelievable, vast, transpersonal "wow" glide through me, like a wave of One der (a mystical form of wonderment).

Eric and his colleagues are taking all of us to the leading edge. Their work demands that they think and act as one single organism with a purpose and a deadline. Eric's skill set includes the ability to bring people together in ways that transcend their personal differences. This is the paradigm shift. In order for our children and grandchildren to flourish, we must act as if this time we are currently living in were our launch window for, as Bucky would say, Utopia or Oblivion.

Our experimental school helped prepare Eric and one thousand other children to think beyond themselves. The current set of challenges for all of humanity requires a radical new approach to education. Eric and his fellow classmates live in a new world, one that is now connected in a new way and one that demands a more expansive definition of who we really are.

Are we all individual separate-thinking things? Is any one individual able to solve a global problem? Does it make sense to teach children to believe that there is one smartest person in the entire school? Do we continue to teach and devise curriculums from the place of already knowing the right answer? Should we at this late date believe that language and logical-mathematical are the primary lines of intelligence that we need to teach our children?

Evolution is no longer moving in ten-thousand-year chunks; it is now moving in nanoseconds. We are currently wired via our computers and cell phones into an organism that is socially evolving faster than anyone can keep up with. This challenges us to find the most powerful tools to enhance humanity's ability to co-operate, invent, strategize, and communicate so that the most nimble of us can discover ways of being that currently do not exist.

MAVEN has already sent back enough data to reveal that there was at one time water on Mars and that the atmosphere was stripped off. There is a very high probability that life exists in other galaxies, but so far what we have learned makes it very clear that our planet is a rare and wonderful place and the only place in our solar system where life has evolved.

The edge of evolution is inside of each one of us. We are both unique and universal. Each of us has the ability to view ourselves from a species perspective. We are here to adapt and invent ways to cope with the complex set of problems that we have helped to create out of a consciousness of infinite, selfish exploitation. When we stand in the place of being an evolutionary co-creator, we can act in a selfless way on behalf of the wonder and majesty of this pretty planet.

Eric and his wife are concerned about their children's education for a good reason. Their options stink. The powerful presence of his two dynamic kids remind him of how much curiosity, energy, playfulness, and wonder they have, and he wants them to retain each one of those qualities as they grow. He experienced the deadliness of his local public school and the aliveness of his time with us, and he wants his kids to have the ardor to co-create a new paradigm.

MAVEN and Juno are inventions and beings that were brought into this world through a new paradigm. It was not profit that motivated this team. It was not individual success. It was not to exploit a resource without any thought of tomorrow. MAVEN and Juno are actualized One ders. These spacecraft are an extension of the best of humanity. By being directly re-lated to these two missions, I have received news from a very different source. This new source was informing me that we are capable of amazing things. Juno entered into its orbit almost to the exact second. It traveled farther and faster than anything we ever made, and it arrived one second after we had planned. MAVEN tells us that Mars was close to being able to support life but not close enough. Mars and Venus tell us every day how lucky we are to live on a planet that is just right.

The Future of the Children

In our present day world, twenty-one-thousand children under the age of five years old die every day. This stunning global fact should be enough to wake us up, yet we continue to live on the banks of denial. What will it take for us to break out of the chains of the dominant worldview that allows us to ignore the alarming rate of species loss that some estimate to be seventy-two every day? Why is education more important at this mo-ment than any other time in human history? I believe that the way we educate our children could be the trim tab that changes the course of human history.

Bucky talked about the narrow edge on the rudder of a huge ocean liner. This trim tab, when moved, created a low pressure that moved the entire rudder and hence guided the ship in a new direction. Which is why his grave stone reads, "Call me Trim Tab."

It was also Bucky who said, "Every child is born a genius. It is my conviction, from having watched a great many babies grow up, that all humanity is born a genius, and then becomes de-geniused very rapidly by unfavorable circumstances and by the frustration of all their built-in capabilities."

I was in my early twenties when I heard him say that, and it became my trim tab. I proceeded to operate as if it were true. I tested it over and over again. First I tested it as a stepparent and parent and then as a teacher. What I discovered along the way was how children respond and grow when they are experienced as geniuses. I used the word "genius" to mean that every child had something powerful to give to all of humanity. I learned to listen deeply to all of the children in my life, and because of that listening I have received the grace of their love.

When we began this journey, I invited you to experience children first as teachers. This simple idea guided me from the moment I heard Bucky. Although my hearing is dimming as I grow older—no more rock concerts for me, thank you very much—my listening is deepening. The older I get the more fascinated I am by relationships. I am currently learning to listen by placing my attention in the consciousness of someone else. Listening deeply is leading me to expand my sense of self, and as I near my seventh decade I feel more alive and vibrant than ever.

Listening and learning from children has allowed me to occupy the next paradigm. In order for us to come into a deep attunement with the natural world, we must expand our consciousness and listen from the place that many indigenous people had access to. It is why we must value every tribe and every aboriginal as sacred. They knew what we have lost.

I read something by Sir Laurens van der Post once where he said that these people were "rich in belonging." It is this beingness that needs to be present when we are listening to our children. Learning from children opened up worlds of possibilities. When we began our school in 1971, we discovered that more was possible than we had ever imagined. By the time we had finished our first decade, we had learned to substitute expectations for possibilities. When we were making the transition from "right answers" to "asking questions," we discovered the brilliance of our minds when we put them together. The only coherent explanation I can give about the success of the school given that I was only twenty-three years old when I first became its director is that it was not me who led; it was us. We intuitively and instinctively leaned into a group mind, which immediately expanded the domain of possibilities.

By the time we fully embraced developmental education, we had learned to experience children and adults as moving through stages of growth. This helped us understand children better, and it helped us to understand ourselves. We were now being guided by something much larger than our thinking-thing mind. We were using leading-edge theories from developmental psychologists and testing them without having to ask anyone's permission. This enabled us to learn from direct experience, and it helped us to attune to each child and to each other.

Our school has always been more tribal than institutional. We began to invent ceremonies, all-school meetings, rites of passage, and passion projects to bring us together and to deepen our bonds. The numinous aspect that had always been with us became more and more apparent as we matured. We even began incorporating the word "spiritual" into our initial interviews. We would answer the question, Do you have any religious affiliation? by saying we were spiritual. Then we would tell them that our common ground was centered around our love of the natural world, our protection of childhood as sacred territory, and our direct experience of the unique gift in every child. We always included every faith and the fact that we embraced agnostics and atheists as well.

By integrating Howard Gardner's theory of multiple intelligences into our culture, we began to deepen our appreciation for inter- and intra-personal intelligence. This was also there from the beginning, but it deepened and expanded as we kept learning and inquiring. We are only just now beginning to realize the importance of inner knowing. This area of inquiry and development is only just emerging. It is, in my view, the edge of the edge of evolution.

We are a wild school, and we were not very long ago wild people. This wildness, this passion for becoming and belonging is what's required to live on the edge of evolution. Our children can lead us there only if we embed them into the context of the Universe Story. They need to know from the inside out where they come from, who they are, why they belong, and how much is at stake. Our children deserve their childhoods and the individual attention that will lead them to their life's purpose and passion. They also need to be imbedded in communities that are much more like eco-villages than gated communities. Our children thrive when they are in a safe, loving community of compassionate humans. They will grow new forms of being and becoming, forms that we are only now beginning to see emerging. These new expanded senses will include deeper listening; deeper seeing; honoring and being led by deeper intuitive sources; deeper feelings for all sentient beings, as well as for mountains, rivers, lakes, and oceans; and deeper entwinements.

If we were to focus on children as our future, we would discover how quickly that investment would lead to new breakthroughs in creative problem-solving. The power of a collective imagination inspired by serving the entire cosmos would create an ever-expanding wave of innovation. If evolution's current is given direct access to children, they will influence their parents, their communities, and they will honor their ancestors, while focusing on building a new kind of relatedness never before seen on Spaceship Earth.

This new tomorrow would be one where human population was stabilized, women would be empowered as the essential drivers of the relatedness revolution, and we would preserve every wild place left on the planet. We would learn to make things last longer, and we would learn from the natural world how to truly re-cycle and re-use. We would stop making toxins and would dedicate vast amounts of time, talent, and treasure to restoring and remediating all of the fresh water systems on the planet. We would learn how to feed ourselves by using methods that honor the soil as the sacred medium of life. We would live within our means and use the sun and wind to power our homes and transportation systems.

Children are change agents. Just ask any parent. Every child born on this planet forces us to change who we are and how we behave. Children learn by watching us. They have the ability to see right through our words and to find all of the contradictions in our actions. The future of our species and of the essential life-support systems of this planet resides in the DNA of each child. We know that even DNA has been tampered with because of the unconscious amount of toxins that we have introduced into our environment.

From 1971 until this current time we have been singing the Beatles song, "All You Need Is Love." It has served us well, but now we need something more than love.

Grace

How do we transform our educational systems from fear-based to love-based? What is our plan of action? How do we stop the degradation of our earth and heal it?

When will we realize and act as if we are One? These questions and others take us to the edge. The edge of what we know and the edge of what we don't know. It is at the vast edge of "what we don't know we don't know" that we are now standing.

Perhaps Evolution's edge is not a place but more of a field of consciousness. Many times before our species have sent scouts right to the shore of a vast body of water, and perhaps each time that lone scout looked out and collapsed in despair. However, we know that as individuals we are really quite unremarkable; it is only when we co-operate in great numbers that the impossible becomes possible. As individuals we could never have sent a solar-powered rocket to Jupiter, but as collaborators we have done just that. When we lean into this collective field, we discover inexplicable connections, experiences, and synchronicities. The more of us who learn how to access this field, the more probable our trim tab becomes.

Grace is something that belongs to divine consciousness. Many of us have experienced it, so we know it exists. Grace for me was being born into a loving family. Grace was growing up in a hamlet of love and abundance. Grace was having Miss Lynn for speech class and receiving my first and only A-plus-plus for speaking from my heart. Grace was learning about Upland Hills Farm School in a Kresge store in Malaga, Spain, from Ken Webster. Grace was falling in love with Karen and Nina. It goes on, and I'm sure it does for you as well.

We, for sure you, are waking up. We often wonder why we're here, what needs doing, how do we find meaning and happiness. We struggle with our problems and work and strive to find this elusive happiness. Perhaps this time more than any other is the gift we've all been waiting for. The world we live in now must change and will change. For those of us awakening, we must do this work together because it is so enormous it will take every ounce of our intellect, imagination, courage, and heart.

It was grace that led me to travel to Carbondale, Illinois, to participate in Bucky's World Game. His vision, the one that called us there, was "to make the world work for 100% of humanity without endangering the natural world." There were only forty of us there that hot, humid summer of 1970. We've been playing it ever since, each in our own way.

I've read some estimates about the number of people on this planet at this time that are entering into or residing in a stage of consciousness that doesn't think we're right or that we even know. Yet this stage can see the partial truth in every stage that preceded it. From this place of not knowing and understanding how important it is to meet people where they are, we can have evolutionary conversations that move us closer together. From this stage we can work together in new ways to change ourselves while we heal our relationships with others and the natural world. If the estimates are even close, say 7% of all of humanity—that's 7% of 7.2 billion people or close to 5 million people—then imagine how quickly we can find our way to that vision of Bucky's, a "world that works." The low pressure will move the trim tab, and the rudder will change course.

The children we have known for these past forty-five years grew in a field that was designed to encourage them to care for each other and for the earth. Our journey of designing , building and sustaining a school have taught us about the importance of creativity. The new beings of this time must be nimble, innovative, adaptable, and creative. They will also have to be connected to the stars. These Upland Hillers are trim tabs. They are multipliers. They are part of a much bigger movement of awakening souls all over the globe, and they are ready to act.

The Stars are calling us now in a new way. They are asking us to go beyond our perceived limitations, to go beyond our self interest, our narrow consumptive habits, our thought prisons and our destructive cataclysmic behaviors. They are asking us to re-invent ourselves as a species.

As a grandparent of five children, I can sense by watching them grow and meeting their friends that there is an amazing new generation of children who are yearning to live lives of meaning and purpose. Each of them and all of their friends, and every other child on this planet at this time, is a sacred child. They are sacred because they are the future. They are sacred because they were delivered to this moment. They are sacred because it is through them that the future of all of life will either flourish or degrade. Our mission is to make sure that they develop and deliver their gift. Our directive is to empower them to connect deeply to each other and to the edge of evolution. Our challenge is to find ways to undo old patterns that were designed for a different time. Our critical path is aimed at becoming wise humans, true homo sapiens who are ready to take responsibility for this precious living earth and the universe. We are more then we ever thought. In this moment we are being called to collaborate not as individuals, not as communities, not as nations, not as stewards of this planet but as the leading edge of consciousness itself.

Epilogue

WHEN HARRY MET BUCKY

When I began this journey that led to being an integral part of a community dedicated to shifting education away from fear and towards love, it was because of the love that I had received during my childhood. My parents were the perfect parents for this middle child. They each contributed something extraordinary that made my childhood a sacred one. My mom taught me by example to do my own thinking and to break any rule that kept me from realizing my true mission. My dad knew how to listen beyond the surface of things. When he was recovering from his heart attack, we bonded in a new way. I sat on his hospital bed and shared my story. I talked about how lost I felt at Michigan State University, about the impersonal size of the required classes, about feeling guilty that I was wasting his money, about marijuana, about Herman Hesse's book *Siddhartha*, about the unjustness of the war in Vietnam, about being cut off from my friends—and all he did was listen without judgment.

Just last week I was driving to Dexter, Michigan, to meet with my friend, editor, and publishing mentor Steve. We were finally completing a book that began before we met in 1972 and that we worked on in earnest during the 1990s. It felt as if I had been almost pregnant for over fifty years.

As I drove from Oxford to Dexter, a memory dropped into my conscious mind. I remembered when I went to a two-week overnight camp in Dexter called Wagon Wheel. I was twelve years old, and this was my second attempt to leave home for two weeks. The first one failed miserably, as I called home only after the second night. I was not only frightened and afraid of leaving home, I was also undone by the camp's military style. We had to stand at attention, march in single file, and follow orders, three things that I was terrible at and that scared me to my core. When my childhood friend and I gathered up enough gumption to ask the camp's director if we could call home, we were summoned to his office and yelled at. My friend called first, and his mother refused to come and pick him up. He was crushed. I called, and my dad drove up that day to get me.

Camp Wagon Wheel was different. First, there was the fact that I had a deep attraction to a neighborhood girl, whose name was Ivy, and she attended the girls' camp Cottonwood, which was on the same property as Wagon Wheel. Ivy loved to climb trees, to draw, and she loved horses. She was an introvert who spoke in images. When she told me that Cottonwood was starting a camp for boys called Wagon Wheel, I took it as the prelude to our possible marriage.

The actual experience of being a camper at Camp Wagon Wheel was that I was a part of a small experiment with only eight boys and a loving couple who lived on the Cottonwood property. We rode horses every day and did simple farm chores. We ate at our house and interacted with the girls very rarely. I loved it. One happy memory imprinted on my mind was when we decided to play polo with croquet mallets and croquet balls. Luckily the horses would have none of it, and we ended up on the ground rolling in manure and laughter.

During the second half of my second week, I was bitten by a tick and ran a high fever. I called dad after the second night of that fever, and he drove up that day to take me home. When we got into the car, I was already feeling better. We started driving in silence, and I was thinking how upset he might be at having to pay for two camps in two summers and me bailing out before either one was finished.

Just when I was going to thank him for collecting me he said, "Let's stop at this corn stand and bring home some fresh Michigan sweet corn for everyone."

After buying two dozen ears of sweet corn, we got back into the Buick. He took my hand, and we rode the rest of the way without talking. My eyes filled with tears of gratitude.

Harry was a gentle man. He was kind, funny, generous, and warm. He was also flawed. He had a loose relationship with the truth, most evident on the golf course when you asked him what he got on the last hole. He kept his worry and his anxiety locked up inside of himself, and he always erred on the side of optimism, refusing to see bankruptcy around the next turn. He at times used sarcasm when talking about mom, and he deflected painful experiences by using humor and wishing the pain would go away. All of these shades of grey made him vulnerable and beautiful at the same time.

What our father and our mother knew was that their children were their reason to be alive. They were born to be parents, and they loved that almost as much as they loved being grandparents. This form of parental love, driven by their full embrace of each one of us, gave us the room to become who we were meant to be. Their joy was most evident around our family dinner table on Friday night. We were given full permission to invite anyone we wanted to dinner, and we did. There were no rules, but there were intuited guidelines. We had to take into consideration how many people could fit around the table, and we learned to improvise to accommodate every guest.

Our mom began cooking days before each meal, thinking of special dishes that each person might like and inventing new ways to make her signature apple pie. She would rarely sit, having eaten steadily while cooking. Her joy was serving others, and she savored that joy while we savored her cooking.

As she attempted to strike a match to light the Sabbath candles, we all paused for a moment as she blessed us by reciting a prayer that she had learned by heart yet would always change by placing a new word here or exchanging another phrase there; like her pie it was never the same. My dad would recite in fluent Hebrew the prayer for the wine in a sweet, song-like voice with such ease and softness that it felt like grace itself was now flowing into our hearts.

When I heard Bucky Fuller say that "every child is a born a genius," it went straight into the center of my being. I have tested it, used it as my true north, and discovered deeper meanings of it as I grew. I have thought about the twelve hours that we spent together. As a man of eighty-five, Bucky was a source of the deepest form of love. He called it metaphysical gravity. He was a direct experience of it. He was curious, humorous, generous, childlike, intense, and very kind. He called himself an average man, and that seemed like the biggest compliment he could give to all of us average people. He was so many things to so many people, but for me he was the greatest teacher I have ever known.

My dad and Bucky got along famously. They both shared something at their deepest core. They loved children. They loved to laugh. They loved to learn, and they acted as if every child was a "sacred child." They experienced children as beings of delight. They transformed in the presence of children and radiated from their insides out. You knew it just by being with them.

They were truly human kindness in form and also the true meaning of humankind. This kindness, this love, is what's needed as we struggle to get out of the grasp of our current, destructive, obsolete paradigm and to embrace a new story, a story based on our love for children, all human children as well as the children of all species. If we are the only species to become self-aware, then we are responsible for all of the damage we have already created and for using our collective effort to create the low pressure that turns us in a new direction.

The night that Harry met Bucky we sat around our dinner table in the house that Bucky named Upland Hills House. Our 1,500 square-foot, passive solar home had just been built, and our kitchen was full of food that Karen had made, having received instructions from Bucky's office manager, Shirley. I don't recall any formal blessing of the meal, but we soon realized that Bucky had impeccable table manners, and somehow that got translated into us eating a bit more slowly with a slight hint of refinement.

Bucky and Harry were sitting on either side of my young daughter Sasha, and they both loved her presence. She was the sacred child. She belonged to the universe, and they knew it, and they communicated it to her through smiles and touch, through jokes and their attention. As the sacred child, she might have sensed that she was being loved for being a child, and so she set the tone for the entire night.

After Bucky dedicated the Upland Hills Ecological Awareness Center, we got back into the car, Bucky in the front seat and Harry in the back seat. I drove my father to his car, and Bucky turned to place his hand on my father's hand. As Harry was getting out of the car, Bucky smiled and told me that he was going to miss Grandpa.

This was the gift of that evening for me. I was about to be challenged with whether or not the school would survive. Soon after that night I would be faced with the school's lowest enrollment, and it would take almost the entire decade for us to get back on course. However, I had something new to add to my medicine pouch. I had something that would carry me through this dark night of the soul. Inside of me there was this growing sense of what a real man could be. I had been taught through example that a real man could be strong enough to cry. A real man could be tender. A real man could be strong enough to thrive after the loss of his child or the loss of his status and livelihood. A real man could get back up and keep trying because there is something that keeps pulling us forward, something mysterious and powerful.

> *The Future of Children depends on us being led by the sacred child.*
> *This sacred child lives in every one of us.*
> *This sacred child lives in the children that have come before us, and the ones who have yet to be born.*
> *This sacred child is not separate from us, she is us.*
> *This sacred child comes through us and yet does not belong to us—she belongs to the Cosmos.*
> *This sacred child is the reason we must change our story.*
> *This sacred child holds the potential for the future that is always pressing into the present.*
> *We must learn to listen to her as she charts a new direction for our species.*

This direction is embedded in a new story. This story began to unfold under the stars just after fire was discovered and our deep ancestors invented language in order to tell it. This new story is deeply connected to those first peoples and to their sense of belonging to the wonder of it all. Yet this new story is also embedded in the new discoveries that are coming to us from deep space probes like Juno and in the science of our genetic makeup that reveals just how deeply related we are to each other.

We shift the course of humanity through deep inter-connectedness when we wake up to the fact that every child matters. Every child is a sacred child. Every child is looking into our eyes asking us to wake up.

PHILLIP MOORE

Phillip Moore began teaching at Upland Hills Farm School in 1971 and served as its director for 42 years. During this time Phil developed a profound learning community for the students, teachers, and board. This culture of curiosity developed into a synergetic collaboration between the staff members that transcended most traditional models of educational institutions.

Moore also led a team to raise 1.5 million dollars and secure 31 acres of land, upon which he led teams to design and build five innovative buildings for their needs. These include a wind-powered Geodesic Dome, a schoolhouse that contains six classrooms, library, and kitchen, a wind and solar powered, sod-roofed Ecological Awareness Center, and a performance theatre that seats 150 people.

Phillip and his wife Karen raised two amazing children both of whom attended the school full term. They are blessed with five wonderful grandchildren.

Now that his tenure as hands-on director of the school has ended, he has begun new ventures of his "re-wirement." This includes developing a team to guide and innovate new education initiatives through his firm Trimtab. Follow Moore's work at www.TrimTab.in.

The children of Upland Hills

Learning at the school garden

Buckminster Fuller (Bucky) (R) and Phil at Upland Hills, 1980

Allegra Fuller (Bucky's daughter) at Upland Hills

Children are empowered when they are engaged

With Ram Dass (R), 2017

Karen & Phillip Moore

Made in the USA
San Bernardino, CA
20 July 2017